God's Trustees

to whom much is given

God's Trustees

to whom much is given

Charles E. Dietze

The Bethany Press

SAINT LOUIS   MISSOURI

Library of Congress Cataloging in Publication Data

Dietze, Charles E   1919-
    God's trustees, to whom much is given.

    Includes bibliographical references.
    1. Stewardship, Christian. I. Title.
BV772.D46   248'.6   75-43848
ISBN 0-8272-1216-X

Scripture quotations, unless otherwise noted, are from the Revised Standard Version of the Bible, copyrighted 1946 and 1952 by the Division of Christian Education, National Council of Churches of Christ in the United States of America, and used by permission.

Cover art by DeVere Shoop

*"Every one to whom much is given,
of him will much be required"*

Luke 12:48

Foreword

It long has been my contention that the churches have done a far better job of teaching the concept of stewardship than many church leaders believe. To be more precise, the teaching of stewardship by the churches probably is the most single important factor behind the tremendous giving by the American people. Every year they give of themselves, of their time, of their skills as well as of their material possessions to a countless number of charitable, philanthropic, and religious causes.

It may be only a slight exaggeration to suggest that the American people profess a deeper and broader understanding of the need of people to give of themselves than is communicated in so many sermons on stewardship.

In this remarkable and readable volume my friend Charles E. Dietze has come forward to help restore the definition of stewardship to its classic definition and to encourage people to reflect on their stewardship as trustees—of life as well as of time, talents, energy, and material possessions.

This is a challenging book. It first challenges the reader to review and enlarge his own operational definition of stewardship. The author next challenges the reader to see himself or herself as a trustee—at home, in the church, and at work. Finally, Dr. Dietze challenges each of us to see the new opportunities to give of ourselves which come in unique forms to each generation.

After reading this volume each of us will be better equipped to live as responsible stewards, to understand our own need to give, and to see new opportunities for fulfilling that need which we were not aware of yesterday.

Lyle E. Schaller
Yokefellow Institute
Richmond, Indiana
November 14, 1975

Preface

Several years ago when I was pastor of First Christian Church in Henderson, Kentucky, we decided to observe Laity Sunday and asked William G. Craig, a young attorney in the congregation, to speak on stewardship. In his sermon he said that he thought of stewardship as being *trusteeship*. He described, in his inimitable fashion, what trusteeship meant to him as an attorney and as a Christian. From that day until now I have felt that that point of view is not only valid, but it has brought deep meaning to my life and ministry. I learned in my study of the scripture that it is just as accurate to translate the words usually translated "steward" and "stewardship" as "trustee" and "trusteeship." Hence the point of view of this book.

Moreover, I have become convinced that this approach is more than a matter of semantics. In Jesus' day, "steward" and "stewardship" had meaning because his contemporaries used the terms in their everyday conversation. A steward was a house manager, an administrator. He was a servant who was entrusted with supervision of his master's property, one who was distinguished by a special position of trust and responsibility. In our day, the words have come to have particular meaning and are used, for the most part, in ecclesiastical settings, similar to the word "deacon." For us, "trustee" and "trusteeship" are not so limited. They are words which have broader meaning in our society. They are more nearly "now" words, especially in legal usage. A donor is the person who provides the gift—the trust—and the trustee is under legal obligation to make the gift grow and produce for the benefit of the beneficiary.

Furthermore, in ecclesiastical circles today, "stewardship" has become so closely associated with money that it has lost what I feel is its biblical and total life meaning. That is not true of "trusteeship." I have asked scores of people what "stewardship" means. With few exceptions, they reply immediately: "money."

The title of this book is more than an attempt to evade old terminology. It is an earnest effort to help us understand that "trusteeship" is a way of putting life all together, of affirming that life *is* a trust. From my point of view, all persons are *not* divided into those who *are* trustees and those who are *not*. Rather, we are all *responsible trustees* or *irresponsible trustees*. Our present ecological "crunch" and our energy crisis demonstrate this judgment which we have brought upon ourselves. They are real and they are frightening. We dare not pretend that they do not exist.

I am grateful to Bill Craig for sharing his insight with me, for helping me to begin to "put it all together." I am equally grateful to my wife, Mary Nettie, and my son, Bill, for their patience while I have been at home writing. They are not accustomed to having me under foot that much because of the nature of my work as a regional minister.

The time to write has been provided by the General Board of the Christian Church (Disciples of Christ) in North Carolina through establishing a policy of educational leave for the members of our staff, a policy being followed now by many of our congregations.

I appreciate very much the encouragement of Sherman Hanson of Bethany Press and W. A. Welsh, president of the Christian Board of Publication, especially for their openness to an untraditional point of view.

A special thanks goes to David F. Marshall of Atlantic Christian College, author and former editor, for many helpful suggestions regarding the manuscript, and to Lyle E. Schaller for writing the Foreword.

Charles E. Dietze
Wilson, North Carolina
June, 1975

Contents

one

Trying to Put It All Together

"How do I know where I'm going if I don't know where I came from?"

"How does anyone expect me to know what I'm going to be (vocation) when I don't know who I am?"

"What's it all about, Charlie?"

These are *now* ways of asking a fundamental question that persons of all ages and of both sexes have been asking for a long time. Most of the literature that has been produced—books, plays, the Bible—as well as most music, art, and religion have, in some way or another, been attempts to "put it all together," to deal with some or all aspects of life and its meaning for persons.

The answers put forth by creative persons have been answers which they have found valid and meaningful in their thinking, reading, encounters with others, and in their own life experiences. How could it be otherwise? Each person in his own way must deal with life as he knows and experiences it day by day. Putting it all together is a continuing process from the time we are born until life is over, no matter how we define what we mean by "when life is over."

Many of the world's religions began because someone appeared on the scene who seemed to have some answers to the meaning of life which in some way made sense to others, who became followers or "converts." That meaning was something with which the followers could identify. It provided answers for *them* in their quest for meaning.

Buddha's teaching of human brotherhood through identification with the suffering of others made sense and still does. It was a life experience for him; for his followers it became a universal truth.

Mohammed's great experience was that life has no meaning without complete submission of one's body and soul to the will of God (Allah). It is strange that most people in the Western world do not realize that the religion of Mohammed is closely akin to Judaism and Christianity because the Moslem gives close attention to the Ten Commandments, especially the first.

Judaism and Christianity, through Moses, the prophets, and, Jesus, teach the love of God and the love of neighbor as central themes on the way to finding meaning in human life. Each of their great teachers and leaders within that broad framework shared particularly meaningful aspects of life's meaning from their own experience, such as Amos' insistence upon justice, Isaiah's emphasis upon the holiness of God, and Micah's call for mercy and steadfast love.

Millions of people have found clues to the meaning of life through these four religions and some through many, many more. In recent times, new religions seem to spring up whenever some person comes up with some different way to put life's answers together. The converts are those for whom the new faith seems to give life new substance. They can identify with it.

Perhaps these new religions are but symptoms of the inconstancy of our times. During the last century, with the rapid expansion of knowledge and the more general availability of higher education, people in the Western world seem to be less and less willing to accept life's meaning from traditional religion. They are looking elsewhere for ways to put their lives together.

Change is so rapid and so constant that anything traditional seems unreal. The character of society these days is such that one has difficulty in finding any meaning in life. We live in an impersonal society, a nonpersonal culture which engenders anxiety and hopelessness. People feel that they are not persons; they seek identity, but have difficulty in finding it. Black people embrace movements that give them some sense of belonging; women fight for their identity through the women's lib movements; even baldheaded men have come up with at least one organization for identification.

Because of the nonpersonal aspects of assembly-line production, automation, credit cards, and many other depersonalizing aspects of our culture, we cry for help and we buy friendship with someone who cares, the psychiatrist. Those of us who cannot afford a psychiatrist or who think we are not ready for him buy books by the millions, and these books are helpful. They help us put it all together better than we have been able to put it together before.

It is hard for us to realize that psychoanalysis, psychotherapy, and their derivitives are products of the last one hundred years. Sigmund Freud began his work in earnest at the turn of this century; much of his contribution to the search for life's meaning is only now becoming apparent. Carl Jung, one of Freud's students, saw the relationship between mental health and healthy religion as he developed his system of analytical psychology.

Increasingly as persons turn to professionals in the field of mental health, the professionals are becoming what might be called "psychotheologians." In their relationships with persons who are suffering from anxiety and hopelessness in a nonpersonal culture, they are developing, testing, and writing about life styles that are helpful in enabling persons to cope with change, to cope with themselves and to find meaning in their relationships with other persons; in short, they are helping persons to put it all together, to find life's meaning.

Among those in this field who have been helpful to me are Viktor E. Frankl, Rollo May, Eric Berne, and Thomas Harris.

Frankl, professor of psychiatry and neurology at the University of Vienna, was a victim of the Nazis at the concentration camps at Auschwitz and Dachau. He is the founder of the theory of *logotherapy* which, he says, "focuses on the meaning of human existence as well as on man's search for such a meaning."[1] He indicates that *logos* is a Greek work that denotes "meaning;" it is the same word translated as *word* in John 1:1: "In the beginning was the *Word* (logos) and the *Word* was with God and the *Word* was God."

"What matters, therefore," Frankl says, "is not the meaning of life in general but rather the specific meaning of a person's life at a given moment."[2] It was this that enabled him to survive the dreadful experiences of the concentration camps. It was his *experience of suffering* which enabled him to find meaning as he endured it.

Rollo May defines religion as the assumption that life has meaning. Religion, or lack of it, is shown not in some intellectual or verbal formulations but in one's total orientation to life. Religion is whatever the individual takes to be his ultimate concern. One's religious attitude is to be found at that point where he has a conviction that there are values in human existence worth living and dying for.[3]

Berne and Harris, although less explicit about the meaning of life, certainly do give some interesting and helpful ways for human beings to learn how to live together in meaningful relationships, ways which they have discovered and tested in their various kinds of therapies.

It is interesting to note that the most recent and definitive book on *sin* was written by a psychiatrist—*Whatever Became of Sin?* by Karl Menninger.

When I noted above that we are experiencing the emergence of "a new breed"—"psychotheologians"—I did not mean to cry "foul." I am simply pointing out that, in our culture, psychiatrists seem to be finding the need to help their patients find some kind of life meaning. For some reason or other, their patients do not seem to be getting it from their traditional source, religion.

Since many psychiatrists and psychotherapists these days are behavioral scientists, they deal more with experiential learning

---

1. Viktor E. Frankl, *Man's Search for Meaning,* ©1959, 1962 by Viktor Frankl, p. 99.
2. *Ibid.,* p. 110.
3. Reprinted from *Man's Search for Himself* by Rollo May. By permission of W. W. Norton and Company, Inc. Copyright 1953 by W. W. Norton and Company, Inc., p. 210.

and therapy than they do with theories. Frankl and May will probably readily admit that much of what they have learned about the meaning of life has been learned in their life experiences as persons. This is not an unusual way to learn our identities, but the importance of this kind of learning is just being discovered. The group emphasis on learning—sharing with small groups who we are as persons and drawing from that experience learnings which enrich our lives—enables us to learn anew that we are who we are precisely because of what we have experienced in our relationships with other persons. The meaning or meanings which life gives us is learnings which we have experienced.

Frederick Buechner has noted the same kind of experience among theologians:

Most theology, like most fiction, is essentially autobiography. Aquinas, Calvin, Barth, Tillich worked out their systems in their own ways . . . and are telling us stories of their lives, and if you press them far enough, even at the most cerebral and forbidding, you find an experience of flesh and blood, a human face smiling or frowning or weeping or covering its eyes before something that happened once . . . may be no more than a child falling sick, a thunderstorm, a dream, and yet it made . . . a difference which no theology can ever entirely convey or entirely conceal.[4]

Let us think back over our lives in our own search to put it all together. What makes sense—what has meaning—to us, in books we have read, sermons or addresses we have heard, conversations and experiences with other persons, plays we have seen, TV programs we have watched? Undoubtedly they were experiences and concepts with which we could identify. They meant something as though they were our experiences. The meaningful experiences which have helped me put together whatever I have put together were of that kind.

When I was in seminary, it was customary for students to take turns speaking in chapel. I must have heard a hundred sermons but I really remember only *one*. Speaking as a student to other students, the young theologue, in 1, 2, 3, traditional homiletical style, admonished us to "1. Know what to say and *say* it;

---

4. From *Alphabet of Grace*, pp. 3-4, by Frederick Briechner. Copyright ©1970 by Frederick Briechner. Used by permission of the publisher.

2. Know what to do and *do* it; 3. Know what to be and *be* it." That is pretty good advice for anybody; that is what putting it all together is all about—seeking to discover what "knowing what to be and *being* it" means to each one of us.

Being a Southerner, I have had problems about my feelings in regard to the War between the States, as I was taught to call it. To me, wars have always been an enigma, an example of man's ultimate folly. I have spent many hours arguing about when war is justified and when it is not. One night many years ago, watching Paul Green's *Wilderness Road* in Berea, Kentucky, I was deeply moved during the scene when the men in blue and the men in grey were spotlighted, alternately, on opposite sides of the stage. The group on one side was praying for victory; the light on that side was dimmed and those on the other side were highlighted. They prayed for victory, too. *Both sides used the same words.* Paul Green accomplished more in one scene than I did in all of my arguments against war.

As a pastor, as a seminary administrator, and as a regional minister, I have come to know hundreds of people in many walks of life. I have learned much from many of them. I met one once, an elder in a student church that I served, who was consistent. He was a farmer in burley tobacco country. He didn't smoke, said he didn't believe in it, so much so that he wouldn't grow tobacco. With the potential profits from tobacco crops, that man's consistency was expensive, but very meaningful.

I was spared the agony of many college students whose inherited faith is shattered by the new ideas and experiences which come during one's encounters as a freshman. During the second semester, I was fortunate enough to be in a creative writing class taught by Professor Ernest W. Delcamp. Some days he would write one word on the blackboard, give us no explanation and instruct us to write. Later, we would discuss in class what we had written, no holds barred. Often he would share some of his unpublished essays or poems with us (he called the latter "verse or worse"). If one of us was struggling with some problem of faith or ideas, we would spend the whole class hour trying to find an answer that was meaningful. We hated to hear the dismissal bell ring.

Then there was John Willie Jones, a churchman, a banker, a political leader. The summer I became his pastor he called me one day and asked me to come by the bank. With the door to his office closed, he told me that he had been chairman of the church board for almost fifty years. Then he said, "But Dietze, I know you have a lot of ideas and I want you to know that, if you think it would be helpful to have another chairman, just let me know and I'll step down. I soon learned that that would be the last request I would want to make because his leadership was brilliant. He was a natural leader from whom I learned much. Upon his death, I discovered that there had been scores of young people who wanted to go to college, but who had had no collateral with which to borrow funds. But "Mr. John Willie" did not turn them down. He simply made them loans out of his own pocket.

Knowing persons like these and sharing such experiences have been meaningful to me and have helped me become who I am. Each one of us has had some similar life experiences.

Is there a common experience of every person with which every other person can identify? Or, to put it another way, is there a completely universal experience that all persons share that may enable all of us to put it all together? I believe there is. In the following chapters we will seek to discover what that common experience is and how it may enable us to put it all together.

two

Life Is a Gift

What are we doing at this moment? What are we doing that every other person, everywhere, is doing now? We are *living*. We have *life*. No matter how we may differ about how or why this is true, it is a common universal fact: *we have life*. Theologians, scientists, historians, sociologists, psychotheologians, doctors, lawyers, Indian chiefs, people who believe in God and people who do not—every person who exists, has existed, and will exist—all *live*.

Where did that life, where does that life, where will that life come from? Again, a common universal fact: *life is given. Life is a gift*. We did not choose it to be so. We could not prevent it from happening. Life is given.

It has been the experience of the vast majority of thinking people throughout history that God is the Giver of life. This, of course, has been particularly true of persons who have found meaning in some form of healthy religion—"healthy" in the sense that their religious *experience* (not just traditional religious beliefs) has enabled them to affirm that life is basically good and can have meaning. Whether or not their religious faith is traditional is not as important to them as whether or not they have found through their experiences some way of finding meaning for their lives.

Rollo May affirms the validity of this kind of religious experience when he points out:

One of the first things necessary for a creative relationship to the inherited wisdom in the religious traditions is to remove religious discussion from such deteriorated forms as the debates over the "belief in the existence of God." The tendency to make that issue central—as though God were an "object" alongside other objects, whose existence can be proved or disproved as we prove or disprove a mathematical proposition or a scientific fact—shows our modern tendency to split up reality. And then, following the dichotomy which Descartes bequeathed to us, we tend to assume that everything must be proven by the methods which properly fit mechanics and physical science.[5]

It is a fact of human experience that persons give their supreme loyalty to something. It is a choice which we make whether we are fully aware of our choice or not. In our time we have witnessed the rise of nationalism as the greatest claim upon loyalty. But we are finding that to be a poor choice. Our nation may demand some part of our loyalty, but it is not worthy of the supreme loyalty. The supreme loyalty can be given only to the one who gives life—God.

It is no wonder that in Judaism, Islam, and Christianity, the *first* commandment is: "You shall have no other gods before me." That was the first and it is the first. It is the beginning of beginnings. It is the supreme fact of the ages. "In the beginning, God," . . . in the end, God and God in all ways and in all things in between. He created the earth, made possible its fruits, and in due season . . . us. He created, he creates, he sustains life—your life, my life. He had the first word and he will have the last word. We experience creation and re-creation day after day—because God gave and continues to give life.

It is no wonder that the Lord's prayer begins with the words, "Our Father." When Jesus spoke the words, he uttered them not

---

5. May, *Man's Search for Himself*, p. 209-210

as a member of a chosen race but as member of one family of God which encompasses all races, all creeds and no creed, all nations, all religions. In the name "Father" he gathered up the whole of humanity into one family. In these words there is nothing exclusive. They symbolize the whole world, and they reach out to every human being, everywhere.

Many years ago when I was in seminary, one of my fellow students was preaching in the chapel and said he always wondered what Jesus meant when he prayed, "Our Father who art *in heaven.* . . ." He said it was the "in heaven" that bothered him, so he suggested that by changing one word he could be more comfortable with the phrase and that he could get far more personal meaning. He indicated that he thought the change would not do injustice to Jesus' meaning. He suggested praying: "Our Father who art in the *universe.*" It does add scope—in the universe, but Father all the same. In the universe, he is God; in the human heart, Father. That has great meaning for me as well. God, our Father, gave me life. It is his gift. He gave you life. It is his gift.

What makes this even more meaningful is my awareness that *I am God's gift to me. And you are God's gift to you.* That puts it where I can experience it. It makes me worth far more than I dare ask.

Jesus put it all together beautifully and meaningfully:

This is why I tell you: do not be worried about the food and drink you need to stay alive, or about clothes for your body. After all, isn't life worth more than food? and isn't the body more than clothes? Look at the birds flying around: they do not plant seeds, gather a harvest, put it in barns; your Father in heaven takes care of them! Aren't you worth much more than birds? Which one of you can live a few more years by worrying about it?

And why worry about clothes? Look how the wild flowers grow: they do not work or make clothes for themselves. But I tell you that not even Solomon, as rich as he was, had clothes as beautiful as one of these flowers. It is God who clothes the wild grass—grass that is here today, gone tomorrow, burned up in the oven. Will he not be all the more sure to clothe you? How little is your faith![6]

---

6. Matthew 6:25-30, From the *Today's English Version of the New Testament.* Copyright ©American Bible Society 1966, 1971. Used by permission.

In *The Celebration of Life,* Norman Cousins engages in an interesting discussion of the possibility of life elsewhere in the universe. Rather than diminish the uniqueness of human life, he says, such a view enhances the importance of the human adventure.

What is most important is that, whatever its place in infinity, life is infinitely precious. . . .

It is precious because the human mind can contemplate such questions as these. We do not have to experience infinity to encompass it.

It is precious because we have access to the phenomenon of cause and effect, thus being able to create our own causes and to shape our own effects. We can dwell on the experiences of past lives and thus enhance our own time.

Life is precious not because it is perfectible but because human beings can comprehend the idea of perfectibility. It is precious because there are no limits to the fineness of human sensitivities. We are capable of responding to the good, the true, and the beautiful. We have the capacity to love and respond to love.

Life is precious because human beings can do things for the first time. We can continue to create in ways we have never created before. We can do the impossible.

Finally, nothing about human life is more precious than that we can define our own purpose and shape our own destiny.[7]

If this is the quality of life that God has given us, then the gift of life brings with it a responsibility for its use. This is not to say that it is a tentative gift; the gift is fully given. But the Giver has some investment in his gift, and although he exacts no return on his investment, he trusts that he will receive some return.

One day many centuries ago an old tentmaker was sitting outside his place of business plying his trade. He was in ancient Ephesus, a thriving center of life and industry. As he worked, three Greeks greeted him and gave him a letter. The letter was from Corinth, and among other things it contained a report of the church there. Some of the members of the church were having trouble following their new faith because of all of the pagan practices which were accepted in their immediate culture. Almost hidden among the answers which he gave to the Corinthians as

---

7. Norman Cousins, *The Celebration of Life* (New York: Harper & Row, Publishers, Inc., 1974), p. 67-68. Used by permission.

he wrote his response is this simple but direct affirmation: "You do not belong to yourselves, but to God. . . ."[8]

Paul was speaking particularly about sexual morality in this instance, but that statement has a much broader meaning. To me it means that I belong to God because he is the Giver of my life. I am God's gift to me. I did not just happen. I came into being because of natural law. God is the source of that. But *he* gave me to me. Therefore, what I do with my life is not just my concern, but God's concern as well.

God gave you to you, so my relationship with you is not only God's concern, but my concern, too.

If the Corinthians had wisdom enough to see that, they could go a long way toward solving their differences.

We see the meaning of this more clearly when we realize that God works his way in the life of the world by allowing persons to be responsible for each other.

We are on our way, then, as we seek to put life all together. The process begins with an affirmation that life is a gift, that God is the Giver of life—your life and my life.

Again, Norman Cousins adds to our search in *The Celebration of Life:*

I would have you consider that the highest purpose of the human species is to justify the gift of life.

We do this in many ways: by being aware of its preciousness and fragility; by developing to the fullest the potentialities and sensitivities that come with life; by putting the whole of our intelligence to work in sustaining and enhancing the conditions that make life possible; by cherishing the human habitat and shielding it from devastation and depletion; by using our free will to the utmost in advancing the cause of life; finally, by celebrating life.[9]

---

8. I Corinthians 6:19b, From *Today's English Version of the New Testament.*
9. Cousins, *The Celebration of Life,* p. 69.

three

Affirming Our Trusteeship

The earth is the Lord's and the fullness thereof,
   the world and those who dwell therein.

—Psalm 24:1

The above affirmation of the psalmist seems to broaden the Apostle Paul's affirmation that we belong to God. Not only do we belong to God but so does the earth and its fruits.

Several years ago, Methodist Bishop Edwin Holt Hughes preached a sermon on "God's Ownership," using the psalmist's affirmation as his text. After worship he went home with a layman who owned a large farm. When they had finished eating a sumptuous meal, Bishop Hughes and the layman spent an hour walking, surveying with their eyes the hundreds of acres of beautiful bluegrass land. As they started up the steps into the lovely old farmhouse with tall Corinthian columns supporting the two-story porch roof, the farmer turned to the bishop and said: "Bishop, in the light of your sermon today, do you mean to say that this land is not really mine? It belonged to my father and his father before him. All of us have had deeds indicating that the property belonged to us." Bishop Hughes, with a twinkle in his eyes, replied: "Ask me that question a hundred years from now."

Another bishop, William Temple, Archbishop of Canterbury, once wrote:

Because we have neglected God, we have also neglected His law. We have forgotten that we are His creatures equally with the other animals and the earth itself. Leaving God out of account we have found ourselves able to utilize all natural resources for our purposes and have regarded ourselves as lords of creation.[10]

Because we have so regarded ourselves as indicated by our present crises in ecology and energy resources, we are experiencing the truth of Temple's indictment.

Edward H. Hume illustrates the concept of trusteeship in African thought:

In this vigorous leader (Chief Albert Luthuli), old African and imported European cultures were fused. Though trained in modern, western ways, yet he was steeped in the thinking of a Zulu tribe. He had felt the best—and the worst—of Western contact with primitive people. "Though I am a native African, yet my country is controlled by Europeans, few of whom recognize that they are here only as trustees. Through all these recent years they have come to think that they own all the land in South Africa."

"Haven't they owned it?" the visitor asked quietly.

"Owned it!" the chief said in surprise. "No, of course not. No one of us *owns* land. It all belongs to our tribes. We chiefs are merely custodians for it. The idea of individual and private ownership of land is wholly foreign to African thought. Land, all of us Africans believe, is to be *used,* not *owned..*"[11]

In ancient Hebrew tradition, the land belonged to God and was entrusted to the people for their use. This is reflected in Psalm 24:1-2:

The earth is the Lord's and the fulness thereof,
   the world and those who dwell therein;

---

10. William Temple, *The Hope of a New World* (Plainview, N.Y.: Books for Librarians, 1940), p. 16.
11. Edward H. Hume, *Doctors Courageous* (New York: Harper & Row Publishers, Inc., 1950), p. 54. Used by permission.

for he has founded it upon the seas,
    and established it upon the rivers.

Samuel Terrien comments upon this passage:

Earth and mankind belong to the God of Israel. "All the earth is mine!" This is the claim of the God who chooses for himself "a peculiar people" (Exod. 19:5-6). And not only the earth, and all that it contains, but also "the world" in its immensity, for Yehweh is creator of the universal nature.[12]

This psalm was part of a liturgy which was probably used in the celebration of the sabbatical year (every seventh year) and the Year of Jubilee (the forty-ninth or fiftieth year at the end of seven sabbatical years) during which the farmers let their fields lie fallow for one year as an expression of gratitude to God for allowing them to use the land.

Leviticus 25, a part of what Old Testament scholars call the "Holiness Code," instructs the ancient Hebrew in the belief that the productive soil belonged to God and was to be used to feed the people and not to be used for personal gain. Verse 23 specifies: "The land shall not be sold in perpetuity, for the land *is* mine." This tradition goes back as far as 561 B.C.

It is my understanding that, according to English Common Law, all of the land "belongs to the king," and "land owners" are granted only a right to use of the land.

Liberty Hyde Bailey has shared his understanding of the concept of deeply motivated conservation by saying:

If God created the earth, so is the earth hallowed; and if it is hallowed, so must we deal with it devotedly and with care that we do not despoil it, and mindful of our relations to all beings that live on it. We are to consider it religiously: Put off thy shoes from thy feet, for the place where thou standest is holy ground.[13]

All of these statements were written over *thirty* years ago. About this same time, there was organized a group called "Friends of the Soil." A pamphlet describing its purpose indicated that it "is a distinctly religious movement founded upon the Lordship of God over man, the earth, and its resources. Its

---

12. Samuel Terrien, *The Psalms and Their Meaning for Today* (New York: The Bobbs-Merrill Co., Inc., 1952), p. 105

13. Liberty Hyde Bailey, *The Holy Earth* (New York: Charles Scribner's Sons, 1916), p 14

purpose is to lead men to regard the earth as holy and man as a steward of the Eternal; to assist the rural church to minister to the total life of the rural community; to work for the reclamation and conservation of the soil and other natural resources and to seek by word and deed to restore man to his divine earth-right to the end that justice may be established on the land and a richer, fuller, and more abundant life may be the lot of all."

As these words are being written, the Congress of the United States is dealing with several bills related to strip mining and other conservation measures. Because we have not willingly been "friends of the soil," we are now being forced to legislate conservation.

Evidently we have been willing to recognize that life is a gift, that the earth and its resources are gifts, but we have not fully accepted the interrelation of the gifts. We have gladly accepted the bounties of the earth and its fruits, but have been unwilling to accept the responsibility to use them wisely for the benefit of all persons.

Perhaps we have accepted the gifts of life as though they were solely ours and not as gifts to be shared mutually with all humankind.

It will be helpful at this point to go back to one of the fundamental teachings in the Hebrew-Christian tradition, a precept equally revered by the Moslems, the eighth commandment: "You shall not steal."

We have usually interpreted this commandment as meaning, since it is a *commandment,* that stealing is wrong. That is to say, we view it merely as a prohibition against stealing because it is in sacred writ. We have wrung out of the commandment all of the ramifications of stealing—stealing goods, services, ideas. So far, so good. But there is more to the commandment than that. *Why* is stealing wrong? Is it just because the commandment says, "You shall not"? Is it because when we steal something from another, we are taking away from him something valuable and thereby depriving him of something of worth? That surely *is* true and deepens our understanding of the teaching.

But there is more: stealing is wrong because *things have inherent human value.* When we steal from another, we not only take away from him the intrinsic value of the object stolen, but we steal that portion of the person's *life* used up in acquiring the object. When we steal things, we steal more—we steal a part of human life and that is unforgivable because human life is precious. Likewise, the sixth commandment, "You shall not kill" is not just a prohibition against taking human life; it speaks to the peril of having an easy conscience about the value of human beings. One of the greatest tragedies of our times is not just that we have taken so many human lives in personal and national conflicts, but that we have done so with an easy conscience.

At this moment we are going through one of the most soul-searching periods in the life of our nation as we evaluate the loss of the war in Vietnam and our involvement in it. Maybe what makes us conscience-stricken in a growing realization that in Vietnam we learned that war is ugly, bemeaning, wasteful, and wrong primarily because human life is good, valuable, and infinitely precious. Our experience there might be one of the most important lessons we have ever had, if we learn it well.

Since life—all life and all lives—is a gift, we are trustees of life, all life; let us, therefore, *affirm our trusteeship of life.* Life is ours; it is a gift, but it is a gift held in trust. We are trustees of life. God is the Giver, but he is the initial and ultimate owner. A trustee is not permitted to do whatever he chooses with a trust. His actions are governed by the owner's desires and intentions. Only God has the first word and the last.

We may be living in a time when this affirmation may have more meaning than ever before in human history. We are becoming "fed up" with war and destruction; we are learning that in order to survive, we *must* become concerned about the value of persons, the conservation of the earth and its resources. This is not a time of hopelessness but a time of soberness and reality, a time of learning, a time of promise and a time of hope—a time of *trust.*

The responsibility is totally ours; that is what a trustee is for: to accept the responsibility of the trust.

four

Whose Time on Our Hands?

Ours is a time-conscious generation, the most time-conscious generation ever to be given a portion of time.

What a way to begin a new day—with the alarm clock screaming in our ears or the radio blaring out all of the horrible news of startling events that happened on the other side of the world while we were sleeping. (When we bought the darn thing, we fell for the salesperson's pitch that it would awaken us to soothing music.) It is now 7 o'clock.

We set the timer on the stove, and in the middle of dressing it pings out the signal that the eggs have been boiled exactly three and a half minutes. A glance at the gadget on our wrist says it's time to hurry. This gadget pulses the seconds just a little faster than the pulse pulses the pulse. We must meet the train or bus or car pool car or hit the road by exactly 7:20 or be late for work. We punch the time clock at 7:59 sharp. We set the wrist watch up a minute or two to be safer tomorrow. The time clock tells us when we work, when we drink coffee, when we eat lunch, when we go back to work, when we drink coffee again, when we get off work, when we start again tomorrow. We hurry home, eat something, in order to be at a meeting at 7:30, then we hurry home in time for the news at 11:00, set the clock so it can scream at us again tomorrow. No wonder many persons die during their first year of retirement. They can't stand the change of pace.

The irony of all this timekeeping is that although we are a time-conscious generation, we are not conscious of the significance of time. We keep time but we lose people. Many of our physicians tell us that heart disease and strokes can often be prevented by the wise use of time. Their main prescription is to slow down. No one really knows how much time is lost and how much of life is wasted by the hectic pace we follow. It results not only in physical diseases but in much of the anxiety and depression which engulf us.

But, we ask ourselves, how can we slow down? Is it just a matter of making up our minds to slow down only to find out that this is an added pressure, another source of being anxious?

Maybe the answer to that question is not an answer, but another question: *Whose* time is on our hands? The writer of the Book of Ecclesiastes hinted at the answer to that when he wrote:
"For everything there is *an appointed time;*
And there is a time for every purpose under the heavens;
A time to be born, and a time to die;
A time for planting, and a time for uprooting;
A time to slay, and a time to heal;
A time to tear down, and a time to rebuild;
A time to weep, and a time to laugh;
A time to mourn, and a time to dance;
A time to scatter stones, and a time to gather stones;
A time to embrace, and a time to refrain from embracing;
A time to seek, and a time to count as lost;
A time to keep, and a time to throw away;
A time to tear, and a time to sew;
A time to keep quiet, and a time to talk;
A time to love, and a time to hate;
A time to make war, and a time for peace."[14]
cd.,—Ecclesiastes 3.1-8

---

14. Reprinted from *The Bible, an American Translation,* by J. M. Powis Smith by permission of The University of Chicago Press. ©1935 by the University of Chicago.

The words in italics suggest that time is a gift. Our experience of life validates that fact. We have time as a part of the gift of life; therefore, like life as a whole, time is a significant part of our trusteeship. It is the context in which we live out the trusteeship of life. Whose time is on our hands? It is God's time.

That puts time in a framework that gives it significance beyond its usual dimensions. That is what Henry David Thoreau probably had in mind about "killing time" when he said, "As if you could kill time without injuring eternity."

I don't think Thoreau meant that we must be busy, busy, busy all of the time. That is part of our problem now. We do not know how to relax. Rather, we must see time as a gift and see it set in eternity. What we do *with* time and *in* time has an eternal quality about it. The recital of the uses of time as suggested by the writer of Ecclesiastes helps to give us perspective. I have heard the words from Ecclesiastes used as justification for the negative elements in the recital, such as "a time to slay," "a time to make war," etc. A time to slay *what?* A time to make war on *what?* Slay men, or slay animals for food? Make war on other human beings or make war on poverty? The writer was seeking to set time in a context, not make prophetic utterances on the uses of time which he listed.

For most of us, time is precious. Time spent doing one thing means little or no time to do something else. What is important at a moment must be judged in terms of what is important in the *long* view, as the use of time which is set in the framework of all time, however long that may be.

I once thought that playing golf was a waste of time, but I have learned that it is a form of exercise which is good for those who are prevented from some other forms of more strenuous exercise. It is a challenging sport to try to beat par, to do so in the company of persons whose companionship I enjoy. It is one sport that a father 41 years older than his son can play with him. I can see my golf time in a total framework of time. Fortunately my wife agrees with me.

I cannot see reading indiscriminately in the same context. So much is being printed these days that we have to be somewhat selective. To read one book means not having time to read another. We all need variety in our reading, but variety with a purpose.

A few years ago some enthusiastic young Christians accepted for themselves the task of trying to reach every person on earth with the Christian gospel. It was their view that by doing so the missionary task of the church would be accomplished in one generation; they would thereby accomplish what all other generations of Christians had failed to do. We cannot deny their enthusiasm, but we might question their shortsightedness. Each generation following them would have to do the same thing all over again.

Many centuries ago an Egyptian pharaoh made the announcement that he had conquered time. He ordered a statue to be erected outside the city of Cairo which later ages called "the Sphinx." When it was completed representatives came from far and near to bow before the pharaoh in homage and admiration. That proud man and all his world proclaimed that he had broken the bondage of time. He boasted that he had made a figure so solid and so huge that even eternity could not destroy it. With the perspective of thousands of years we look back on the king and smile. His sphinx is still standing but its face is being eroded year after year, century after century. It still stands, however, as a symbol of our finiteness.

Percy Bysshe Shelley showed the irony of the pharaoh's concept of time in his *Ozymandias:*

I met a traveler from an antique land
Who said: Two vast and trunkless legs of stone
Stand in the desert. Near them, on the sand,
Half sunk, a shattered visage lies; whose frown,
And wrinkled lip, and sneer of cold command,
Tell that its sculptor well those passions read
Which yet survive, stamped on these lifeless things,
The hand that mocked them, and the heart that fed:
And on the pedestal these words appear:
'My name is Ozymandias, King of Kings:
Look on my works, ye Mighty, and despair!'
Nothing beside remains. Round the decay
Of that colossal wreck, boundless and bare
The lone and level sands stretch far away.

Only God, the Giver of time, is infinite.

One of the finest discussions on the trusteeship of time is given by Rollo May in his *Man's Search for Himself.* He entitles his eighth chapter: "Man, the Transcender of Time." His discourse is so thorough and meaningful that I do not want to summarize it, but I dare not omit in this context some of his more salient thoughts:

Psychologically and spiritually, man does not live by the clock alone. His time, rather, depends on the *significance* of the event . . . Psychological time is not the sheer passage of time as such, but the *meaning* of the experience, that is, what is significant for the person's hopes, anxiety, growth.

. . . .

The more a person is able to direct his life consciously, the more he can use time for constructive benefits.

. . . .

Hence, it follows that the best way to meet the anxiety about growing old is to make sure one at the moment is fully alive.

. . . .

The first thing necessary for a constructive dealing with time is to learn to live in the reality of the present moment. . . . This is why in therapy "experiencing" is always more powerful and curative than talking *about* experiences . . .

. . . Eternity is not a given quantity of time: it transcends time. Eternity is the qualitative significance of time. One doesn't have to identify the experience of listening to music with the theological meaning of eternity to realize that in music—or in love, or in any work which proceeds from one's inner integrity—that the "eternal" is a way of relating to life, not a succession of "tomorrows."

The question of which age we live in is irrelevant. . . . The basic question is how the individual, in his own awareness of himself and the period he lives in, is able through his decisions to attain inner freedom and to live according to his own inner integrity. . . .[15]

It has always been interesting to me that on two occasions when two men came to Jesus asking the same question: "What must I do to inherit eternal life?" (Mark 10:17-22 and Luke 10:25-37), Jesus answered by giving each one an admonition about living *now.* To the rich young ruler, Jesus said, "Go, sell what you have, and give to the poor." To the lawyer, Jesus told the story of the good Samaritan and added: "Go and do

---

15. May, *Man's Search for Himself,* pp. 254-277.

likewise." According to Jesus, eternity begins now, where we are, with whoever we are at any given moment. Time makes demands of us that we dare not dodge now because it is a time set in the context of eternity.

God's time is on our hands, a portion of which he gives us. We are trustees of time. What we do with it is as much God's concern as it is ours.

five

Using Our Gifts

To say that human life is precious is to affirm the value of human life; to say that *I* am precious is to affirm my value and uniqueness as a person.

But first, how do we arrive at values? Are they precepts that we learn from a teacher in a formal setting? Are they rules of human behavior that we memorize and then act upon? Are they truths which we claim because they are in the Bible—"the Bible tells me so?" To some extent we learn values in all of these ways. But basically our *values* have been learned out of our life experiences, the thoughts, feelings, happenings that we freely choose from various alternatives and which are meaningful to us.

My wife and I are trainers in a program of marriage communication/enrichment. One of the exercises we often use is a values auction in which each participant is "given" $2,000 which he may use to buy, at auction, a number of valuable items which run the gamut from a chance to be the world's richest person to a chance to rid the world of prejudice. It often turns out that if the purchaser is to buy what he really wants and values most, he must bid on only one item and pay the entire $2,000 for it. It is a revealing exercise because it helps each participant to see what his real values are. After the auction he compares his findings with those of his mate so that they can understand better what each other's values are and if there is any serious conflict in values between them. If they get into an in-depth discussion about why they cherish certain values, then they often discover that their values are "caught" from relationships with others rather than learned by precept.

Values are learned early in life, more often "caught" from parents, teachers, associates than learned from more formal ways of learning. Sometimes the values caught are the opposite of what we observe in the behavior of others. I remember a teenager who was an adamant believer in total abstinence from alcoholic beverages because he had seen his father and mother torn apart by the father's alcoholism. No one had to teach this youth the value of abstinence; he learned its value from his own life experience as a part of a home where the disease of alcoholism made life unbearable.

We are all unique persons with values which are probably quite different from the values of others. Of course, we hold some values in common because our life experiences have brought us to the same value choice. But we arrive at individual values because we are unique persons. No one else has the identical experiences in life that we have.

Some of us have learned this fact of our uniqueness because of experiences that we have had in sensitivity or encounter groups. In this setting in small groups where persons share openly with each other their feelings of who they are as persons and draw from that experience learnings which enrich their lives, many of us have discovered that sometimes the only help that we can get comes from another person who risks himself for *our growth*. He gives a part of himself, usually a unique part of himself. In such a setting we often find out what *love* really is—not a declaration, but as Rollo May defines it, *"a delight in the presence of the other person and an affirming of his value and development as much as one's own."*[16]

A parent who really loves his children does not love them because they just happen to be thrown together in a family relationship, or because parents have an obligation to love their children, but because their children are unique persons whose value and development are affirmed by the parent as much as the parent affirms his own value and development.

We are precious human beings because God has given us life; but he has given us unique life through allowing us to be ourselves, to be peculiarly *us*.

There is, however, more, much more to our uniqueness. Each of us has unique gifts. Some of us can sing, some can dance, some can write, some can act, some can farm, some can build houses, some can serve in unique fashion. All of us look different, sound differently, act differently. Otherwise, those who do impersonations would have to do something else as a vocation.

Whatever our unique gifts are, they are *abilities* which God gives us to enable us to be peculiarly ourselves. They are qualities of life which empower us to perform in particularly unique ways. Thus, there is only one Bing Crosby, one Bob Hope, one Jackie Robinson, one Chris Evert, one you, one me.

Abilities are unique gifts because they are *our* abilities. Others may perform similarly to the way we perform, but when we perform, it is peculiarly our way of performing. This makes life interesting because our encounter with every other person thus becomes a unique encounter for that person and for us. Our abilities are a significant part of God's gift of life to each one of us as a kind of one time, very personal endowment.

Although we differ in our abilities, we are equal in our responsibility to use whatever abilities we have for the welfare of all of us. God didn't make only you or only me. He made us both and he made every other human being on earth. Our trusteeship is a *mutual trusteeship*. Our gifts are for the welfare of all persons. Because we are endowed with our peculiar gifts, we are responsible for using them for the welfare of each other, for the welfare of all.

---

16. May, *Man's Search for Himself,* p. 241.

40

In our society an affirmation of mutual responsibility is hard to understand because we have been programmed to compete. Most of the problems we face in international relations, in church squabbles, in economic conflicts, in family relations, in generation "gaps," in social and racial inequalities, in sexist attitudes—are the result of our *not* affirming our mutuality and interdependence as human beings. In all of the areas of human conflict these days everyone clamors for his rights, but few plead for responsibility and mutuality. We all have gifts, abilities, which are needed by all mankind. To use them for ourselves alone is to cause them to lose much if not most of their value.

There is a radio and TV spot announcement which says: "A mind is a terrible thing to waste. . . . Support the United Negro College Fund." I have heard it dozens of times, but it always jars me to new awareness of our human mutuality. We might long since have had a cure for cancer if prejudice had not kept some brilliant black person from expanding his native ability in college or university to become another creative scientist like George Washington Carver. By whatever means, keeping another person from using his gifts to the fullest is to take away from him and from society his potential gifts for the welfare of all.

Using our gifts, then, is a significant part of putting it all together.

A few years ago we were shocked at the news that Fritz Kreisler, noted and gifted violinist, had been seriously hurt in an automobile accident. When he recovered after a long illness, he appeared at Carnegie Hall for his first concert after the accident. A great audience was there to hear him. Many of his friends felt that he should not have attempted to give the concert. Some of them thought that the recital would only reflect how much of his former skill he had lost. But as he began to play, all of their doubts subsided; he still had retained his own genius. At the conclusion of the performance he received one of the greatest ovations ever heard at Carnegie Hall. Later that evening, when he was told of the fears of his friends, he declared that the renewed talent and power to play the violin did not belong to him. He said simply, but clearly, that he felt that he was an agent—a trustee—through whom God was able to bring music to the people.

six

Words and Human Welfare

Words! Words! Words!
Like harmless bullets
fired at my brain.
God words! Big words!
Bible words! Church words!
Long words! Lost words!

I've learned the words
and used the words
and memorized the words
until I'm full of words.
They're plastered across my brain
like stickers in a billboard.

But they're only words.
I don't know what they mean

or where they belong.
I can't fit them into a conversation
. . . unless I'm swearing.

At school they never say
redemption
or grace or sanctification.
The teacher doesn't seem to think
that words like sacrament
or Holy Ghost
really mean as much
as history
or the vitamin content
of eggs on toast.

Words are everywhere.
People spit them out
all the time
and most of the time
they are wasted.
There are millions of words
spinning through the air,
millions of sound waves
crashing against each other
and saying nothing!

Lord,
is there one word,
one word strong enough
to get through all the other words
and reach me?

Is there a word that can
get under my skin
and reach me
and change me?

Is there one word
with a face and hands

and power and life,
one word I can meet head-on?

Is there one word
that will not fall through
the cracks into my subconscious
and die?
Is there one word like that?
One solid word?
Is there?[17]

There are times when all of us feel like that. From the first "Good morning" at the beginning of the day until the last "Good night" as we crawl into bed, we spend our waking hours in a steady stream of *words*. All day long we hear words, speak words, sing words, read words, write words. They come so easily. We can't live without them. Sometimes I wish I could do as my mother used to do—turn them off! (She had a hearing aid.)

Nevertheless, words are important. They are, as S. I. Hayakawa put it, "*. . . the essential instruments of man's humanity.*"[18] The power of speech is a gift, another gift from God. Words are products of that gift, and we are trustees of them.

The ninth commandment is not "You shall not bear false witness" but "You shall not bear false witness *against your neighbor.*" Lying is wrong, according to the ninth commandment because it harms *persons*. In Deuteronomy 19:15-21 we discover that it was regarded by the ancient Hebrews as a crime for a witness to lie in order to aid in the conviction of another person. Such "false witness" was considered so serious a crime that anyone found guilty of falsifying evidence was punished by receiving the same penalty that would be given to the convicted defendant.

Words have moral significance because human welfare depends upon our moral use of words. Although words in

---

17. From *For Mature Adults Only,* by Norman C. Habel (Philadelphia Fortress Press, 1969), ©1969 by Norman C. Habel. Reprinted with the permission of the publisher, p. 92.
18. S. I. Hayakawa, *Language in Thought and Action* (New York: Harcourt, Brace, Jovanovich, p. 261.

44

themselves are neither good nor bad, moral nor immoral, they have moral or immoral significance in the way we use them. When Thomas Mann said, "Speech is civilization itself," he was getting at the human value of words.

Decent human relationships *depend* upon truthfulness. In a society which respects truthfulness, we know where we stand. If falsification were the rule rather than the exception, none of us would know where we stand. We could never be sure of anything, what time it is or what anyone else really is saying.

Many years ago, E. Stanley Jones defined Christian speech as that speech which answers affirmatively these three questions: (1) Is it true? (2) Is it kindly? (3) Is it necessary? We usually limit the test of responsible speech to the first question only. The implications of the two other tests would take us too far afield here, but they certainly are worthy of testing. How about the *brutal* truth? We all know about the times when some statements are better left unsaid. The wordiness of our times has conditioned us *not* to hear what we are saying to each other.

Fortunately, however, we are beginning to develop better ways of communicating with and understanding each other. Basically, these are really ways of "checking out" what we think we hear another person saying. Some call this "active listening," whereby the hearer repeats, in his own words, what he thinks he heard. If the message was received correctly, then all is o.k. If not, the speaker can repeat in different words what he was trying to say. This kind of clarification results in better communication and better understanding.

For the most part, words are symbols of feelings. What we need to communicate through words is how we feel because feelings are real while words can sometimes mask how we feel. Humans are feeling persons, and true communication is at the feeling level.

Thomas Gordon, author of *Parent Effectiveness Training* and founder of a movement to improve communication between parents and children, suggests "I messages" as a way of improving communication. "I messages" are messages from a person who identifies where he is (how he feels) and are more oriented to the *sender* rather than the receiver. This self-disclosure does not put the receiver on the defensive and most often elicits a positive response from the one to whom the message is sent. Instead of saying, "You brat! Don't you ever pick up your clothes?" his mother says, "It makes me angry to see clothes spread all over the house." The clothes dropper is much more likely to pick up (or not drop) clothes with this positive kind of comment. Many generation-communication gaps are being bridged by such methods.

We are also learning that some of the most significant communication is not through words at all, but through body language. The scientific study of body language, *kinesics,* indicates that what we do with our bodies in conversation often communicates a completely different message from that which we think we are communicating with words.[19]

The movements of our bodies express how we honestly feel. Psychiatrists are learning to use body language as a tool for helping patients discover what really is "bugging" them.[20] It can help all of us understand ourselves and others more completely.

Intimacy and *touching* are becoming less and less taboo. The connotations of these words are beginning to have a broader and more acceptable meaning.[21] We are learning that we all need stroking once in a while, that children in institutions starve for an occasional embrace. From time to time words like these begin to communicate something quite different from what they once meant.

On one occasion Jesus said something quite strange about the way we speak of each other: "Woe unto you, when all men speak well of you, for so their fathers did to the false prophets." (Luke 6:26) He seemed to be saying that there are times when praise *condemns.* This is the danger which often faces persons of good will who speak out boldly for truth, justice, or freedom. The enemies of such qualities of life sing the praises of those who champion them in order to cover up their own lack of commitment to them. Their real feelings often show in their body language. The trouble is that many public figures are coached by professionals to watch their body language in public appearances.

It is risky for all of us to talk, but it is often more risky not to.

Words are gifts; they reveal the quality of our trusteeship of persons, of things, of ourselves.

---

19. *See* Julius East, *Body Language* (New York: M. Evans Co., 1971) p. 9.
20. *Ibid.,* p. 174.
21. *See* Desmond Morris, *Intimate Behavior* (New York: Random House, 1971).

seven

A Symbol of Life

In one of Giovanni Guareschi's novels about a very earthy Italian parish priest, Father Don Camillo engages in frequent conversations with the figure of Christ on the altar. One day the padre rushes into the church to inform Christ of a gift which will enable him to buy a new Gertrude, the priest's pet name for the bell in the tower of the church. This is their chat:

"The Signora Carolina is going to give all the money needed for casting a new Gertrude!"

"And how did she come to think of it?" [The altar Christ asks.]

"She said she made a vow," explained Don Camillo, "to the effect that if the Lord helped her to bring off a certain business deal, she would give a bell to the church. Thanks to You, the deal was successful and within a month's time Gertrude will once more lift her voice to Heaven! I am going now to order the candle, for the thank offering."

Christ checked Don Camillo just as he was taking off under full steam. "No candle, Don Camillo," Christ said severely. "No candle."

"But why?"

"Because I do not deserve it," replied Christ. "I have given the Signora Carolina no help of any kind in her affairs. If I were to intervene in such matters, the winner would bless Me while the loser would justifiably curse Me. If you happen to find a purse of money, I have not made you find it, because I did not cause your neighbor to lose it. You had better light your candle in front of the middleman who helped the Signora Carolina make a profit of nine million. I am no middleman."[22]

In this experience, Don Camillo follows the human tendency to expect God's values to be the same as his values, but he finds that he is mistaken. This assumption is most often related to money matters, as in the case of the Signora Carolina.

A favorite saying is, "Money is the root of all evil." It is quoted as an eternal truth because it is "in the Bible," but it is *not* in the Bible. The saying is a *mis*quotation of the biblical passage, 1 Timothy 6:10: "For the *love* of money is the root of all evils; it is through this craving that some have wandered away from the faith and pierced their hearts with many pangs." We find the statement in one of Paul's admonitions to his young minister-friend, Timothy, in a passage that deals with the values of godliness, faith, love, steadfastness, and gentleness, with the "love of money" as a deterrent to those ideals.

Money, in itself, is not evil. Money is simply a symbol; it is a symbol of worth, a measure of material value. An article, a piece of land, a jewel, is *worth* so many dollars and cents. This is true in our present culture; it has not always been true. Before money was used, people bartered in other goods which had value. Some people foresee a moneyless society in the future with all transactions taking place by computers without the circulation of bills and coins.

Yet money is more than a symbol of material value. Money has *human* value. It is a *symbol of life.* Money indicates the time, talents, brainpower that is *spent* in earning it. Money therefore represents the life that is used up in earning it. A person who argues about paying taxes as "taking my life's blood" is literally

---

22. Giovanni Guareschi, *The Little World of Don Camillo* (New York: Farrar, Straus & Givroux, Inc., 1951), pp. 167-168.

right, though somewhat shortsighted. When we buy a pair of shoes, a car, a home or anything else, we are also exchanging a part of our life for them, the part that we have used up to earn the money with which to buy them.

Because money is a symbol of life and a symbol of value, it is a particularly useful means of expressing our trusteeship. Life is a gift; we are trustees of life. Money is a symbol of that life; therefore there is nothing more universal than money as a means of expressing our trusteeship. Rather than a mockery (because so many of us tend to worship money more than what it symbolizes), the motto "in God we trust" does have great meaning for those who are honest enough to affirm their trusteeship. E. Stanley Jones calls attention to:

a demonstration in American history of two attitudes toward money and how they have worked out. In 1852 two sets of caravans with covered wagons started out from Omaha across the wide expanses toward the Far West. For days they went in parallel lines, and then they diverged in more ways than one. The Mormons had written on their wagons: "God-seekers." The other group, who represented the gold rush, put on their wagons: "Gold-seekers." The latter group was individualistic, competitive, with the attitude: "Each man for himself, and the devil take the hindmost." The former group was a society of mutual aid, seeking the good of all and of each. These two outlooks and attitudes were put under life to see which one life would approve of. The "gold-seekers" found their gold, but it went through their fingers like water. Their gold is now, for the most part, in the hands of corporations. The God-seekers settled on barren salt land, developed it, and now have a corporation for the good of the whole with assets listed at \$3,500,000,000. Life approved of a society of mutual aid and doomed a ruthlessly selfish society.[23]

Once on a Sunday in Lexington, Kentucky, I came out of church with a friend who remarked: "You know, I had a remarkable experience in church today. It was during the *offering*. . . ." Seeing my startled expression at his comment, he continued: "All of my life I have gone to worship and thought, oftentimes during the Lord's Supper, that there must be some special way I could express my gratitude to God for what he has done for me, some way I could give my life as Jesus gave his. And the

---

23. E. Stanley Jones, *Abundant Living* (Nashville: Abingdon Press, 1942), p. 302. Used by permission.

answer came today because this was the first time I have ever been to a church where the offering immediately follows, as a part of, the observance of the Lord's Supper. As the offering plate came to me and I started to make my gift, I thought, 'That is how I can give my life day after day . . . as I spend my time, talents, and life in making money which I can give. In giving money, I am constantly giving *myself*.' " On the way home I thought, "I had a remarkable experience at church today, too. It happened on the way out."

That particular downtown church has found new life and renewal in the last few years. It has done so, among other ways, by having its members make a Time-Talent Commitment in addition to a money commitment as a part of its annual commitment program. Literally tens of thousands of hours are given each year to empower its significant program of community service in downtown Lexington.

Arnaud C. Marts, founder of Marts and Lundy, Inc., one of the most significant professional fund-raising organizations in our nation, has noted that *"the Church is the chief agency which systematically tries to teach people to give. . . . It is the Church which almost alone carries the burden of persuading people to give unselfishly and systematically to altruistic activities. Religion is truly the mother of philanthropy."*[24]

Since I know Dr. Marts to be a very open-minded person I do not hesitate to question his use of the word *burden*. I prefer *trusteeship* as an alternate. As a churchman I am happy that the church carries the trusteeship of persuading people to give unselfishly because giving is one important means by which persons grow—in their personal fulfillment, in their relationship with God, and in their relationships with other persons.

I have found that sometimes by taking a look at something other than the matter at hand we can understand better what we are trying to deal with. This may be especially true in our consideration of money as a symbol of life and a means of expressing our gratitude to God for all of his gifts.

Let us look at an experience of King David of Israel.

---

24. Arnaud C. Marts, *Philanthropy's Role in Civilization* (New York: Harper & Row, Publishers, Inc., 1953), p. 79.

He had led his men into battle in a very crucial war. The enemy, with overpowering strength, had driven back the forces under David's leadership. Almost surrounded by enemy forces, David and his men were short of food and water. Wearied by the heat of the battle, David expressed a forlorn desire for a drink of water from the well at Jerusalem. Two common soldiers overheard him. At great danger to themselves, they made their way through enemy lines, and under cover of darkness, they approached the well. At dawn, they were back at the front with some of the water for the king. David was deeply moved by the incident and he responded to the brave deed: "But he would not drink of it; he poured it out to the the LORD." (2 Samuel 23:16.)

Akin to the experience of David was that of George Washington Carver as reported by Rackham Holt:

At the beginning of 1933, when banks were crashing all over the country, including the two in Tuskegee and the one at Ames in which Dr. Carver still kept an account, someone was kind enough to be concerned over his savings and inquired as to whether he knew the banks had failed. "Yes," he replied. "I heard about it. All I have is in those three. I guess somebody found a use for the money. I wasn't using it." He had lost something like forty thousand dollars, but beyond making this statement he never discussed the matter.[25]

Although Carver made no decision to "pour out the water," he evidently viewed his savings as not his alone.

Elton Trueblood recalls an experience of G. C. Studdert-Kennedy which shaped Kennedy's view of money:

. . . This modern prophet said that the real meaning of money was brought home to him when he saw a girl dying of tuberculosis while she lived "in one of those abominable pigsties which do duty for houses for a considerable portion of the population." The girl *could* get well, but only on one condition: somebody had to find enough money to transport her to a decent place where she could have fresh air, professional care and good food. Studdert-Kennedy went out and got the money and then he knew, he said, what money is. "It is the power to demand a human service and to be sure that you will get it."[26]

Money is a symbol, a symbol of life. It is a symbol of that part of life which is spent in earning it; of life that is spent in exchange

25. Rackham Holt, *George Washington Carver* (New York: Doubleday & Co., Inc., 1943), p. 301.
26. Elton Trueblood, *Foundations for Reconstruction,* (New York: Harper & Row, Publishers, Inc., 1946), p. 81.

for goods and services; of life that is given to God or for the well-being of other persons. When we give money, we give a part of ourselves.

I once visited a trustee of a theological school who shared with me the fact that he was running his business just to make enough money to pay his taxes on his investment income. He confided that his net worth was nearly a million dollars. He said his goal was to reach the million-dollar figure so that he could bequeath that amount to the seminary for the education of ministers. "Just think," he said, "by doing so, the influence of my life will be multiplied by the influence of every student who receives his education as a beneficiary of the scholarship fund which I will establish!

It became clear to me at that moment that here was a man who was indeed a *trustee,* that his trusteeship represented not only his understanding of the human value of money, but indicated, as well, his belief that through money one may multiply his trusteeship through others who benefit from it.

To give money as a way to give ourselves seems impersonal when we first think about it, but it is not impersonal when we see ourselves as a part of one or more communities of trustees. The trustee mentioned above was part of such a community, but there are many other such communities of trustees.

eight

Communities of Trustees:
(1) At Home

Several years ago when TV was just beginning to become popular, one TV sales pitch was that television would "seal the broken circles of our homes," and "make home the center of American life once more." There were pictures of whole families sitting around the boob tube as though it were a kind of family worship center, with bottles of soft drinks or bottles of wine with trays of cheese and crackers as new elements in a new type of family celebration of holy communion. The mental image we conjured up was nostalgic and, of course, we all bought TV's. But the togetherness never happened unless after watching some pertinent documentary one member of the family was bold enough to suggest turning off the gadget and discussing the content and meaning of what the group had viewed.

Then we got sold on having our own *personal* TV's so we could view what especially appealed to us as individuals.

Discussions about TV center mostly on who should have got the Emmy awards, or on the commercials. I get the impression that the ad writers would make better writers than the writers of the main fare. I seem to remember the ads better than the featured program even though I have trouble remembering the products.

I am convinced that no gadgets, clever as they are, are going to make home life better, because homes are people and only people are going to help persons grow as individuals and with each other.

I submit that what our homes need we already have. They have *us*. When one member of the family discovers some helpful clue to better relationships, he should be given the right by the rest of the family to share what he has learned; and he has the responsibility to do so.

Reading a book like this or any other book which gives some clues to a better way to "put it all together" can be shared with the rest of the family as a gift.

Even more than sharing what we read is sharing experiences which are peculiarly our own. When we do that, we often discover that all of us have had similar experiences. Teenagers are often surprised to learn that what has just happened to them has happened to their parents at some time or other, too.

Sharing ideas and experiences paves the way for building *trust* relationships, and building trust relationships at home is one of the most important growing edges the home can provide. If a growing child does not learn that he is trusted at home and that he can trust the members of his family, he is going to miss something vitally important to him throughout his life.

Nena and George O'Neill have described two kinds of trust in an open marriage, *static trust* and *open trust:*

Static trust is based on expectations and reasonably assured predictability. We count on people to keep their promises, to pay their bills and to keep their appointments. Static trust is absolutely necessary for cooperation anywhere, but since it is based solely on the expectable, and predictable, it does not easily accommodate change.[27]

Open trust implies a degree of intimacy, honesty and openness far beyond what is possible in static trust. To be so open means believing in your mate's ability and willingness to cherish and respect *your* honesty

27. From *Open Marriage*, A New Life Style for Couples by Nena O'Neill and George O'Neill. Copyright ©1972 by Nena O'Neill and George O'Neill. Reprinted by permission of the publisher, M. Evans and Co., Inc. New York, N.Y. 10017.

and *your* open communications. A friend defined this kind of trust by saying, "Trust is the feeling that no matter what you do or say you are not going to be criticized—it is an open policy of not having to keep embarrassing secrets, and the willingness to say what is in your mind knowing that the other person isn't going to use it against you later on. This is trusting *in* someone, not just trusting him. We can be naked in the presence of the other not just physically but in a real intimacy of thoughts and feelings. The idea is that we know we are not perfect, but we also know we are not going to be faulted for what we are."[28]

We do not learn for ourselves how to trust because we "ought" to trust each other, nor do our children learn to trust us and other persons by being admonished to do so. Trust grows out of life experiences in which we respond to faithfulness, upon our learning that we can be certain that some things happen in a predictable manner. Armin Grams points this out by alluding to the fact that "To be a faithful adult means to be one whom others can rely on, one who takes his promises and vows seriously and is inwardly propelled to fulfill his obligations."[29] He illustrates the relationship between faithfulness and trust in this way:

The parable of the prodigal illustrates well the relationship between faithfulness and trust. We are impressed by the decision of this headstrong youth to return home after he had trampled on all that his father held precious. Most of us would have had reservations about such a move, might have had some second thoughts about going home. What made the difference? Why did he decide to go? No doubt the character of his father is the principal factor in the son's behavior. The boy had lived with faithfulness throughout his childhood. He had learned to trust. He was sure that regardless of the circumstances he could count on his father to be concerned, to care.[30]

This illustrates again that we catch values more than we learn them in other ways.

What we have been saying in the context of trusteeship is that trustees of life are those who are trustworthy and to whom others may respond with faithfulness.

One of the most interesting and helpful developments in recent years in regard to human relations is that we are learning that *conflict* is not only acceptable, but that it can be constructive, es-

---

28. *Ibid.*, p. 234.
29. From *The Christian Encounters Changes in Family Life* by Armin Grams, ©1968 by Concordia Publishing House. Used by permission, p. 102.
30. *Ibid.*

pecially in family relationships. We have all engaged in conflict, but we often pretend that it doesn't happen. We push it back into a closet or under a bed or simply lie about it. Not long ago I was in the company of a couple who had been married for forty years and one of them said, "We've been married forty years and we've never had a cross word or a fight." I am glad they were not looking at me when they said it because I was thinking (and I'm sure my facial expression would have indicated my thoughts): "Those two people are either two of the best straight-faced liars I've ever met or they have been bored to death for forty years."

Conflicts are real; they are a part of life; they can be helpful. George R. Bach and Peter Wyden have written *The Intimate Enemy*. Its subtitle is *How to fight fair in love and marriage*. The book is as honest as its subtitle. As marriage counselors, Bach and Wyden have discovered, as they say somewhat in paradox, "couples who fight together are couples who stay together—provided they know how to fight properly."[31] Their book is about how to do just that. Their major point, it seems to me is that "Intimates *trust* each other. They are not afraid that their partners will exploit their weaknesses. They take turns at giving and taking but are not concerned with contractlike reciprocity. They tactfully respect each other's belt lines and temper their honesty with infinite tact so that a partner will not be cruelly hurt."[32] Their clue to success in dealing with conflict is *intimacy*, from which they feel all humanity stands to benefit. I recommend that my readers read *The Intimate Enemy* before they have their next fight. It might be more fun.

Others are coming up with conflict management which changes an "I win, you lose" or "You win, I lose" situation into a "We both win" experience which can make conflict not only manageable but a healthy growing experience. Am I suggesting a "trusteeship of conflict"? It is an interesting possibility.

Our world is changing so fast that it is difficult for all of us to keep up with what is going on *in us,* to say nothing of the external changes that are taking place or the changes that are taking place in our children. It is difficult for us adults to realize how rapidly things are moving. Back in 1962 Dean Harold K. Schill-

---

31. George R. Bach and Peter Wyden, *The Intimate Enemy* (New York: William Morrow and Company, 1968), p. 17. Used by permission.
32. *Ibid.,* p. 325

ing of Pennsylvania State University addressed the Annual Meeting of the Division of Christian Education of the National Council of Churches in St. Louis on "The Explosion of Knowledge." Among other things he said:

When my grandparents went to school they acquired skills that were quite adequate for them throughout their lives. The world in which they died was in most essentials the world into which they had been born.

My father on the other hand lived in at least two worlds. During his life the geographic map, political alignments, economic and social mores and systems, as well as man's physical modes of existence were scrambled to such an extent that he felt that the world of his age was *very* different from that of his youth.

Now my generation has already lived in three worlds. The first was the world of the horse and buggy, the steam locomotive, coal and kerosene, and ice refrigerators. The second was the world of the automobile and the Diesel engine, the airplane, and electricity. The third is that of the atom and nucleus, of space exploration, and of automation. But these three worlds have been recognizably different not only technologically, but in the fundamental knowledge and the ways of thinking that characterized them. Referring to my own field, physics, in my school days it was still predomininantly Newtonian. When I was in college and graduate school, it was Einsteinian. Now it is definitely post-Einsteinian, characterized predominantly by quantum mechanics.

Now there are already on the horizon clouds, as yet but small, that seem to indicate the coming of a storm of new ideas, that may usher in what will be for me a fourth world of physics. . . .

. . . So accelerated has been this growth that of all the scientists who have ever lived, nearly ninety per cent are still alive.

Now let us pause to ask this question. If around 1900 men lived at the rate of one world per lifetime, and by 1925 at the rate of two, and by 1945 or 1950 at the rate of three, and if our children and students are already living at the rate of at least four very different worlds per lifetime, what will be the situation in the year 2000, when many of today's youth will be in their prime? . . .

If a child were born potentially able to solve problems a thousand times more difficult in a thousandth of the time required by an ordinary child we would marvel and be tempted to say that something new had emerged in the evolution of man. But, I suggest, that this has already happened. The generation now being born will in this sense be a virtually new species, because its ability to think, analyze, predict, decide, and create will be tremendously amplified by thinking machines.[33]

Schilling then catalogues some unprecedented changes and unprecedented problems—overpopulation, problems in the area of ideals and values, of ethics and morals, the deliberate manipulation of minds, bodies, and characters of unborn children or of children and adults already living.

He then switches roles from a reporter/forecaster to a churchman to ask in all candor:

How are youth to decide which components of the faith they should hang on to as eternal, and which ones they should be prepared to relinquish at the proper time because they are not eternal?

Schilling does not attempt to answer the question. How could he? Nor can we adults or youth today answer that question except to deal with each single, specific question that arises among us at home, at school, or at church in a trustworthy, honest manner, in intimate, sharing experiences as persons who affirm their trusteeship of all of the life that God gives. These "youth" of which he speaks are *our* children, not some theoretical brood. They, we, all of us are a part of the community of trustees we now call "home." As we recognize that the life of each is a precious gift from God, respect each other's worth and personhood, are willing to share with and to learn from each other, the answers will come as we need them.

Where can we test our mutual trusteeship better than in the close relationships we have at home? If it is not meaningful in that setting, there is little likelihood that our trusteeship will have meaning in our broader relationships in the church and in the rest of society.

---

33. Harold K. Schilling, excerpts from an address on "The Explosion of Knowledge," delivered to the 1962 meeting of the Division of Christian Education, the National Council of the Churches of Christ in the U.S.A., Hotel Sheraton-Jefferson, St. Louis, February 12, 1962. Used by permission.

nine

Communities of Trustees:
(2) In the Church

Throughout its history the church has been called by many names, described in various ways—in biblical terms, in sociological language, in ecclesiological nomenclature. Biblically, the church is "the body of Christ," "the bride of Christ," "the fellowship of the saints," "the called-out society," "the temple of God," "the house of God," "the kingdom of God," etc. Sociologically, the church is "the community of believers," "the congregation," "the society of the faithful," "the company of the committed," etc. Ecclesiologically, it is "a church," "a temple," "a mosque," "a meetinghouse," "a tabernacle," "a cathedral," "a basilica," "a churchhouse," "a synagogue," "a chapel," "a shrine," "a sanctuary," etc.

In the thought of the average person, a church is a *place*, a *building*, a particular *location*. Generally speaking, however, biblical usage indicates some kind of community or fellowship. It is a group of persons bound together by a common purpose or goal or manner of life. It is, as the Quakers call it, "a society of friends."

For our present purpose the church is a *community of trustees,* a partnership of persons who affirm a mutual trusteeship of all of the gifts of God: human life, all life, the earth, the fruits of the earth, the abilities which God gives in differing measure to all persons, the time which it is our privilege to use—the portion of eternity which is allotted to us.

To view the church in this way should help us eliminate some of the "hang-ups" which many of us have regarding the church. A community of trustees may or may not have a building; a community of trustees may or may not have a preacher; a community of trustees conceives its task as that of nurturing *servants* rather than being *served.*

Recently Robert K. Greenleaf wrote a fascinating and prophetic monograph entitled *The Servant as Leader,* one of a series aimed at helping us find some answers to the dearth of leadership which nearly everyone sees as one of the greatest needs of our time.

Greenleaf's starting point, he says, came out of his reading Herman Hesse's *Journey to the East.*

In this story we see a band of men in a mythical journey, probably Hesse's own journey. The central figure of the story is Leo who accompanies the party as the *servant* who does their menial chores, but who also sustains them with his spirit and his song. He is a person of extraordinary presence. All goes well until Leo disappears. Then the group falls into disarray and the journey is abandoned. They cannot make it without the servant Leo. The narrator, one of the party, after some years of wandering finds Leo and is taken into the Order that had sponsored the journey. There he discovers that Leo, whom he had known first as *servant,* was in fact the titular head of the Order, its guiding spirit, a great and noble *leader.*

One can muse on what Hesse was trying to say when he wrote this story. We know that most of his fiction was autobiographical, that he led a tortured life, and that *Journey to the East* suggests a turn toward the serenity he achieved in his old age. There has been much speculation by critics on Hesse's life and work, some of it centering on this story which they find the most puzzling. But to me, this story clearly says—*the great leader is seen as servant first,* and that simple fact is the key to his greatness. Leo was actually the leader all of the time, but he was servant first because that was what he was, *deep down inside.* Leadership was bestowed upon a man who was by nature a servant. It was something given, or assumed, that could be taken away. His servant nature was the real man, not bestowed, not assumed, and not to be taken away. He was servant first . . . "[34]

. . . if one is *servant,* either leader or follower, one is always searching, listening, expecting. . . .[35]

Greenleaf expands his thesis of the servant as leader in another essay, *The Institution as Servant:*

THIS IS MY THESIS: caring for persons, the more able and the less able serving each other, is the rock upon which a good society is built. Whereas, until recently, caring was largely man-to-man, now most of it is mediated through institutions—often large, complex, powerful, impersonal; not always competent; sometimes corrupt. If a better society is to be built, one that is more just and more loving, one that provides greater creative opportunity for its people, then the most open course is to *raise both the capacity to serve and the very performance as servant* of existing major institutions by new regenerative forces operating within them.[36]

I have quoted Greenleaf at great length (although not really enough to give his full thesis and argument) because I understand him to be saying that in our present predicament we do not lack leaders, but we lack persons who are willing to become servants in order for them to be adequate leaders. To me, *this is what the church should really be about.* Because of our trusteeship, our servanthood as recipients of the gifts of God, we need a community of trusteeship like the church to create and nurture such servants. We beget them and nurture them in our homes; we test our trusteeship and expand it through the church. Then as servant/trustees who have found nurture, commitment, and experience as trustee/servants at home and in the church we are equipped to witness our servanthood/trusteeship in the other institutions in society.

What I am suggesting is not some farfetched ideal that is unattainable, because I already see it at work to some degree in the organization through which I serve. Earlier I mentioned

---

34. Robert K. Greenleaf, *The Servant as Leader,* p. 1. Copyright 1972-1973 by Robert K. Greenleaf; reproduced by permission.
35. *Ibid.,* p. 3.
36. Greenleaf, *The Institution as Servant,* p. 1. Copyright 1972-1973 by Robert K. Greenleaf; reproduced by permission.

marriage communication/enrichment laboratories in which my wife and I participate. But we are not *the leaders*. The leaders are two lay couples who serve as trainer/coordinators in a program across our state, North Carolina. They are servant/trustees who have become leaders because of their commitment and training. There is another couple who are servant/trustees who are making a unique contribution in parent-teen communication experiences which are helping to bridge the generation/communication gap.

Daily I am learning from a host of servant/trustees who are rising from the ranks to lead in areas where our regional church staff has neither the time, the expertise, nor the experience to serve as well.

The human resources for able servants with potential to lead are all around us, in the church and outside the church. I yearn for the church to be a community of trustees where these people have a chance to *be* trustees in community, where the strength of one is the strength of all, and the strength of all is added to the strength of the one.

In our present society (and in the church) people in power are afraid of the risk of allowing servant/trustees to become leaders. I do not blame *them* because they have been conditioned by an aggressive, competitive system that conceives power as a value which is higher than serving. Practically everyone wants to be called a "leader." In a community of servant/trustees no one cares who is leader. Leadership may shift from one moment to the next, depending upon which of the servant/trustees has something to contribute to the welfare of the community, not just to *his* will-to-power. In fact, in such a community the will-to-power is displaced by the will-to-serve.

The church must take its share of the blame for allowing the will-to-power syndrome to get into its life and to foster it in society. But in every age there have been communities of trustees which have broken the pattern and become servant communities, such as Clarence Jordan's Koinonia Farm near Americus, Georgia. The risk of such a venture, however, is greater than the average church member is willing to take. But people like Jane Addams, Albert Schweitzer, Kagawa, and others whom the church remembers most warmly among its servant-saints are symbols of that kind of trusteeship.

It has always been interesting to me how the church has denuded the word "service," in spite of the fact that Jesus used that concept widely as a characteristic of a true "son of God." He said:

Whoever would be great among you must be your servant, and whoever would be first among you must be your slave; even as the Son of man came not to be served but to serve. . . .—Matthew 26-28

In every case that I can remember in the New Testament, the word "minister" is used as a verb, as a synonym for "serve." And "ministry" is used to indicate the vocation of every follower of Christ, not just the vocation of a pastor. The New Testament word most often translated "steward" can just as readily be translated "trustee" and really means a type of servant, albeit a kind of head servant—servant, nevertheless.

In the church we speak of the "worship *service*." In doing so we may have made worship a *substitute* for the kind of service Jesus spoke about. Officers in the church "serve" as stewards, deacons, elders, trustees,—service *in* the church, not service in the world as servants of the church.

Evidently in the church we have turned service *inward*, rather than *outward*. Even the word "deacon" which means servant, too, is usually thought of as meaning one who serves only in the church.

I do not mean to imply that such "service" is bemeaning or unimportant. I raise the issue only to point out the limitations we have imposed upon the servant words in the New Testament.

In the context of trusteeship, servanthood is not only implied; it is explicit. A trustee receives the gifts of God; through his trusteeship he serves to *fulfill* his trusteeship.

The role of trusteeship is particularly expressed through giving. Since money is a symbol of life and, when we give money, we give a part of the life we have spent in earning it, gifts of money to the work and service of the community of trustees are particularly meaningful. Giving money is a kind of "double giving," in that we give something of material value and we give a part of ourselves which is symbolized by the money.

Above and elsewhere we have called attention to the human value of money because of life spent in earning it. In the same context, a church budget has a human value content in it. We do not give to a church budget to "pay the preacher"; we provide for the needs of a person who is called to be the shepherd of the trustees in the trustee community; we do not pay the utility bills only; we provide heat, light, and comfort for persons; we do not just buy "literature," we provide the educational tools by which the trustees learn more about the faith; we do not give to missions, we share the faith, heal the sick, provide self-help tools and education for people who have these needs in the town where we live, across the nation, and around the world. A church budget, therefore, is an instrument through which we demonstrate our care for *persons*. As my friend on the steps of the church said, "Money is one way of giving a part of me to express my care for others."

Paul Tournier puts it meaningfully:

This is what the meaning of gifts among mankind reveals to us: Men need to give because they need to give themselves, and all their gifts are signs of that deep-seated and universal desire to give oneself. To live is to commit oneself.

. . . The meaning of gifts is in the love that they express, the love both given and received. All men have this need to give their affection and to feel that it is appreciated. All are equally seeking proofs of their being loved, and of feeling that those who love them have great pleasure in this. We do not want a totally impersonal love; it would only be a dry and humiliating act of charity. Mutuality is the very law of love: There is no pleasure in loving unless the other enjoys equally his being loved.[37]

Several years ago when I was vice-president of a seminary and spent a lot of my time helping to raise funds to keep the institution alive, I frequently called on a lady of retirement age who had been very generous in her giving. On my last visit with her I told her it would probably be the last time I would see her for a while because I was going to a new job. As I stood at the door to leave, she said, "You know, I think I'm in love with you. You have been the only person in a long time who seems to care about me. Will you kiss me good-bye?" After I kissed her and left, I thought of all the lonely people I had met during my ten years in that role, and I thought of the thousands of dollars they had committed to an *institution* because the institution's representative was the only one who seemed to them to care about them. (I've confessed

---

37. From *The Meaning of Gifts* by Paul Tournier pp. 56-57. ©1963 by M. E. Bratcher. Used by permission of John Knox Press.

64

to my wife that this sweet little old lady was the only one I kissed in the line of duty!)

Harold L. Lunger recalls an experience of Harry B. McCormick, former president of the United Christian Missionary Society of the Christian Church (Disciples of Christ) who:

> . . . told of an experience in one of his early pastorates. He happened to be standing by as the officers of the congregation opened the envelopes given in a special missionary offering. All were surprised to find that the largest gift was from a single woman who was the sole support of an invalid mother. The elders said, "This woman cannot afford to give this much." Dr. McCormick took her check and went to talk with her about it. He explained that she had given more than she could afford, and that the church could not accept it.
>
> After listening to his statement, the woman explained, "My daily work is hard and dull—especially since, as a girl, I had my heart set on going to a foreign field as a missionary. But then my mother became ill, and I had to go to work to support her. I am glad to be able to provide and care for her. But the thing that gives me real meaning to my working hours is the thought that I am able, by my giving, to help somebody else go overseas and serve as a missionary. You cannot take away from me this one great joy in my life by refusing to accept my check."[38]

A couple's class in a rural church I once served decided that we needed an addition to the church building, space for community activities. The church board was reluctant to have a fund-raising program, so the class started a "Lord's Acre" project whereby interested persons would grow a crop, raise a calf, or engage in some other project, the income from which would be given to the building fund. One man decided to raise a thoroughbred calf. We planned a "harvest Sunday" when the gifts would be brought and dedicated. The man who raised the calf brought his check, but after worship he took me aside and said to me, "Preacher, I've learned something about giving this week. When I sold that calf, the check was nearly four times as much as I usually give to the church every year. From now on, I'll be giving more to the church. I didn't realize until now how ungrateful I've been for all the Lord has done for me. I've been giving him a 'tip' instead of showing him I'm grateful for his help in my whole farming operation." Others in the church must have learned something,

---

38. Harold L. Lunger, *Finding Holy Ground* (St. Louis: The Bethany Press pp. 40-41).

too, because from that time forward our church giving increased considerably.

Books on giving list, analyze, and categorize motives for giving. I have no quarrel to pick with them. For me, however, there is one motive above all: I need to give in order to express to God my gratitude for his gift of life. I *am* because he gave and continues to give. It is great to be a part of a community of trustees at home and in the church where we can put our gifts together to accomplish so much more than I could accomplish alone.

There are also other communities of trustees in which we may share.

ten

Communities of Trustees:
(3) At Work

It is the purpose of these chapters on communities of trustees to enable us to see more clearly that our search for meaning is not only a personal search, but a mutual one. Not only are we individuals of worth in the sight of God who gives us life and value, but we are bound together in communities of worth which enable us to affirm our personal dignity and to find meaning in the totality of God's creation.

We have found that in our families and in the church we are involved in two specific kinds of communities which enable us to find that mutuality and a sense of wholeness, because these close-knit communities foster a sense of "belonging." In them we feel that we "belong" to something larger than ourselves.

In our society we spend much more of our time, energy, and abilities in another life experience than we spend at home and in the church. We spend them at work.

For many of us work is viewed as a necessary evil, something which we are required by life to do in order to be able merely to survive. Mondays are dreadful days because on Mondays we must "go back to the old salt mine," and face five or six days of drudgery. In our industrial society that point of view is understandable. There is little that is exciting or meaningful about performing the same task on an assembly line day in and day out, week in and week out, month in and month out, year after year after year. No wonder we seek escape from its monotony. Because of the economic necessity for adequate income to live comfortably, many of today's women choose to work outside the home. Housework is monotonous and boring, too. The trouble is that many women go to work in order to escape the monotony of housework only to discover that piecework in a textile plant or another kind of factory simply brings on another kind of monotony.

In our society many men and women work at more than one job in order to earn enough money to provide the means to escape the boredom that their jobs produce. Recreation vehicles of all kinds, "package weekends" at motels and other means of escaping the boredom of work are all a part of the attempt to escape the *meaninglessness* of work.

However, when we affirm our trusteeship of life, work can be more than drudgery; it can become a true vocation.

As Elton Trueblood puts it:

If ours is God's world, any true work for the improvement of man's life is a sacred task and should be undertaken with this aspect in mind. We sometimes suggest this by our frequent use of the word "vocation," but we have used the word so long that we have forgotten the degree to which it is a specifically Christian word. If we can recover the original meaning of vocation we shall be doing something important for our present world.

We have made much of the phrase "full-time Christian service," thereby referring to the priesthood, the ministry and to definite missionary work. The supposition is that people are called to these as they are not called to other occupations. Our rule in this matter must be, "not less but more." Instead of full-time Christian service, we shall do well to speak of "full-life Christian service." The really crucial decision comes, not when a person decides to be a foreign missionary rather than a farmer; the really crucial decision comes when a man decides that he will live his whole life in what the late Thomas Kelly called "Holy

Obedience.'' Whether that leads to farming or banking or evangelistic work in Africa is then wholly secondary. The major decision has already been made and the decision is that to allow one's entire life to be a channel of divine love. This, whatever our work may be, involves a break with a merely secular order. If we were to take our religion seriously we should see the ordination to the priesthood as a sacrament; but we should likewise see ordination to any worth-while human task as a sacrament. It is just as important for one boy to decide to be a Christian businessman as it is for another boy to decide to become a Christian clergyman. If we mark the latter step with special ceremonies of recognition, why should we not mark the former in a similar way? The most damaging criticism which thoughtful young people make of so much current religion is not that it is *untrue,* but that it is *irrelevant.* It is so tangential to life that whether it is true or not makes no real difference. But if our religion is united with the major steps of life, that is, the decisive ones, it ceases to seem either abstract or irrelevant. *No religion is irrelevant if it helps people to see the hidden glory of the common things they do.*[39]

Increasing numbers of young people are choosing the professions as their vocations because they can feel that through their work they are doing something which has human value more readily than going into work in which they merely produce things. But when we affirm the trusteeship of all of life, we can look upon our work as producing things that *persons* use. Because we have not taught our children the *human value of things,* we elevate the value of some kinds of work, such as services, far above the value of producing goods which meet different needs of the same persons who receive the services.

Kenneth Kuntz, in his *Wooden Challices,* quotes the following from a letter from a laborer in an automobile plant:

"I work on the assembly line for one of the great car manufacturers. I operate an electric appliance all day, putting bolts and nuts in the body of the cars. The work is humdrum. My work became really meaningful when my minister helped me see that I was helping provide people with good transportation so they could do their work better and live more pleasant lives. . . ."[40]

---

39. Elton Trueblood, *The Common Ventures of Life* (New York: Harper & Row, Publishers, Inc., 1949), pp. 85-86. Used by permission.
40. Kenneth Kuntz, *Wooden Chalices* (St. Louis: The Bethany Press, 1963), p. 146.

There are some persons, by native ability, experience, and training, who are particularly suited to working with their hands. There is nothing bemeaning about that. They are good at what they do; they do it well. If one chooses to do that kind of work rather than another kind, he is fulfilling his trusteeship of life. He is mature enough to do what he is capable of doing and chooses to do it. It is his *choosing* of his goals that marks his maturity. Rollo May underscores the importance of choosing one's values when he writes:

> . . . Knowing what one wants is simply the elemental form of what in the maturing person is the ability to choose one's own values. The mark of a mature man is that his living is integrated around self-chosen goals: he knows what he wants, no longer simply as a child wants ice cream but as the grown person plans and works toward a creative love relationship or toward business achievement or what not. He loves the members of his family not because he has been thrown together with them by accident of birth but because he finds them lovable and chooses to love them; and *he works not merely from automatic routine, but because he consciously believes in the value of what he is doing.*[41]

When I was a small boy my father worked as "utility man" for a large cotton oil company in Savannah, Georgia. He had come to the United States from Germany with his mother and several brothers and a sister. His stepfather had run through whatever funds the family had when they arrived, so the boys went to work early to support their mother when their stepfather died. Lack of education forced the boys to take jobs for the unskilled, hence my father later became the "utility man" at the cotton oil company. One of his jobs was to clean up the laboratory where the company chemists were working on uses for the by-products of the plant.

My father had a curious nature and often got into conversation with the chemists. They told him they were trying to work out a process to make something marketable out of the cotton seed oil residue. They showed him some of the basic chemistry involved and he often stayed after working hours to watch them complete some chemical procedure in which they were engaged. One Christmas vacation when the chemists were on leave, my father was cleaning the lab and decided to try out an idea he had about

---

41. May, *Man's Search for Himself,* p. 176.

70

the process. It worked! The result was a process for making soap out of one of the by-products of the plant. He told me the story many times, and what I still remember about it is the joy he found—not in perfecting the process, but in the comradeship he and the chemists had. They were part of a *community*. They shared with one another, they cared for each other.

Several years ago it was my privilege to be on the faculty of a Christian Youth Fellowship Conference when these conferences were designed on the "committee plan." I was counselor of the Service Committee. Meeting on the grounds at the same time our conference was in session was a group of about 20 Quaker youth who were engaged in a work camp. Most of these youth were from large cities in the Northeast and their fathers were, for the most part, executives of large corporations. The purpose of the work camp was to add another room onto one-room mountain schools to make possible a lunch program.

When we arrived at the conference, we learned about their program and our committee asked their director if we could join their group for two or three hours each afternoon to help with the construction. We enjoyed the work and the fellowship of their group. We soon learned, however, that their group seemed to accomplish more than our group and their girls complained less about blisters and callouses on their hands. Before the week was over we discovered the reason for the differences in the attitudes of the groups. Each morning before breakfast their group would meet for a couple of hours in Quaker fashion to contemplate the meaning of work, and sometimes they would share quietly with each what the work meant to them as persons and as a group. It was their deeper understanding of the meaning of work in community which made the experience more meaningful to them.

There can be that kind of community in any kind of work when persons who work together have respect and care for each other, when they see the mutuality of their work and its ultimate good for those who will benefit by their labor. Sometimes the only close relationships that some people have is their work relationships. If they do not find warmth, caring, and closeness there, they will not find it elsewhere.

Rollo May, albeit in a different context, speaks of the importance of community, and his statement has relevance here:

Community can be defined simply as a group in which free conversation can take place. Community is where I can share my innermost thoughts, bring out the depths of my own feelings, and know they will be understood. These days there is a great search for community, partly because our human experience of community has largely evaporated and we are lonely.[42]

That is to say, we all need some kind of community where we can be heard, where we can express our deepest feelings and find a comradeship of caring. We need to work at finding it or creating it at home, in the church, and at work.

"Communities" are not limited to home, church, and work, however. A community is not a place; it is not a gathering; community is more of a spirit which pervades a group of two or more persons in the manner described above by Rollo May. Sometimes the most effective communities are composed of those who gather together in a college dormitory, a fraternity or sorority house. They can grow out of a coffee "klatch" or a bridge club. The fact that we gather in small groups is an indication of our need for being with others. Whether or not such gatherings become "communities" depends upon what happens to and among the persons present.

We will not find or create such communities unless we ourselves are willing to risk being persons who are open, caring, willing to listen. Attitudes are just as contagious as values. When we walk into an office, a factory, a home, or a church, the way we are received or responded to often is determined by ourselves. If we smile at the others, we are likely to get a smile in return. If we are grouchy, we are likely to be responded to in similar fashion.

On several occasions recently I have tried a little experiment. As I walk down the street or go into a place of business, I smile at the persons whose eyes meet mine. In most cases I am responded to in the same fashion. If I greet them with a frown, I get a frown in return. It is amazing how much fun it is to see the face of another change expression in response to our own behavior.

Creating positive responses from other persons most often begins with us. If we are pleasant and caring, generally others will respond in the same way. If the other person does not re-

<hr>

42. Reprinted from *Power and Innocence* by Rolla May, pp. 247-248. By permission of W. W. Norton & Company, Inc. Copyright ©1972 by Rollo May.

spond positively, then we can be fairly certain that something is really bothering him. That may open the door for us to be helpful by choosing a more opportune time to engage the other person in conversation when he can really get off his chest what's bothering him.

There are a lot of lonely people around these days. They are hungering for a genuine smile or a signal of caring of some sort. We can begin to *create* community by initiating positive, caring attitudes ourselves. We all need to work at creating a comradeship of caring at home, in the church, at work and in other groups of which we are a part. When we create it, we taste the mutuality of our trusteeship as human beings who live and work for the welfare of all.

eleven

Two Bonus Gifts of Time

Our generation is unique in many ways, not the least of which is that, of all the generations which have ever lived, we have been given *two bonus gifts of time:* nonworking time and time in retirement.

For the most part, our parents and grandparents worked from dawn until dusk, most of them on farms where the father seemed to toil endlessly day after day doing the chores which filled nearly every waking moment and the mother kept as full a schedule pursuing her seemingly endless tasks. There were few gadgets to ease the burdens of work. Cows were milked by hand; crops were sown and harvested without the benefit of labor-saving machinery; bread and butter were made, not bought; fruits and vegetables and meat were raised, harvested, and preserved; clothing was *hand*made; barns were built by the farmer and his neighbors, not contracted by skilled carpenters; a man worked in the fields or in the house as soon as he was strong enough to share a part of the family workload; he retired only when he was incapacitated. Holidays were seldom observed, except Sundays which were a welcome respite and Christmas, the observance of which often required extra work for days in advance of its coming. But even on Sundays and Christmas, some chores such as milking, watering, and feeding the cows and the other animals still had to be done.

To many of today's children and youth the above recital seems like a fairy tale, although many of their parents remember that kind of life only too well. They have difficulty in contemplating life without "wheels," radio, television, weekends at the beach, quick travel in automobiles or jet planes. When we recall the "old days," they sit and listen with countenances of almost disbelief. In those days there seemed to be time only for work and sleep. The Genesis story of Cain's chastisement to earn his living by "the sweat of his brow" seemed very real because most people experienced that manner of living every day of their lives. Free time was only for the rich who owned enough land to hire the hands to get the work done while they hunted, fished, or otherwise engaged themselves in what the workers called "idle pursuits."

What a contrast is the above to Stephen C. Rose's somewhat startling picture of the future:

The estimate is that Americans will have over 600 *billion* more hours of free time in the year 2000 than they now have. Machines and computers will eliminate the need for most semi-skilled workers (from typesetters to stenographers to junior accountants) not to mention the factory laborers who could be replaced *even today* at considerable saving to the companies involved. There will be jobs for teachers, doctors, and other professionals. Business will need men to manage the machines. Wives will still have to push the right buttons and diaper their infant children. But, yes, there will be more free time than our grandparents ever dreamed of. Workers used to strike to gain a shorter work week. Today we can envision unions fighting to maintain the right to work. The sheer abundance of free time will be experienced mostly by our children and by *their* children . . .[43]

What in the world are we going to do with all that time? For one thing, we need to recognize a different *concept* of time. Is

43. Stephen C. Rose, *Who's Killing the Church?* p. 96. Used by permission of the author.

time just an "event in eternity?" Is it something that is measured in specific intervals—seconds, minutes, hours, days, months, years, decades, centuries, millenniums, eons?

In chapter four we called attention to Rollo May's discussion of psychological time as being that which depends upon the significance of events which happen in time, the meaning of the *experiences* for our growth as persons. That concept of time is relevant here. What we choose to do with the bonus gifts of time will determine whether or not the gifts are assets or liabilities.

It has been my observation that some persons who lead busy lives often do not know what to do with free time. They pace the floor, hunt for something to do—anything just to get busy again. They do not seem to be able to relax and enjoy any free time which they have. I have something of this problem myself, but I am working on solutions by developing the hobbies of playing golf and working in my woodworking shop. At least once a month I make a trip by plane and find myself playing the "hurry-and-wait" game that all air travelers know so well. I have found the waiting times and flying times opportunities to catch up on my reading. Nearly every trip now gives me a chance to read one or two books that I cannot seem to find time to read at home. Since I make many trips by automobile I find that by keeping the car radio off except for occasional news broadcasts, I have opportunities to sort things out and ponder anew who I am and where I am going as a person. We all need such time for ourselves.

Hobbies in which we use our hands often give us opportunities to free our minds from the usual pressures and anxieties that engulf us. To feel the velvety smoothness of a piece of wood which we have shaped and sanded into a form which has use for ourselves or for others is therapeutic and gives us the satisfaction of creativity.

Elton Trueblood suggests that

Happiness . . . comes chiefly by some productive art, a working in the way of excellence. Our happiest moments are not those in which we ask how to be happy, but rather those in which we so lose ourselves in some creative task, which seems to us important, that we forget to take our own emotional pulse. . . .
Creative production ought to be within the realm of possibility for every human being and probably is, if we learn to seek it intelligently.

. . . One of the most enviable men I have ever seen was an old man in North Carolina with a sorghum mill. He had a wonderful pride in taking the juice of cane stalks and turning it into sorghum almost as clear as honey. He had found a chance to *create,* in the production of excellent sorghum. Consequently, he was both an artist and a man.[44]

To wait until we retire to develop creative and meaningful hobbies or crafts is to put an extra burden upon ourselves as we make the adjustment from a busy life to one where we have all the time in the world. For some retired persons, finding ways to fill the time is not only burdensome, but it is psychologically unhealthy. If possible, we should begin to *plan* our retirement just as carefully as we plan any other life experience.

One of the blessings of my life has been to know William Clayton Bower. Onetime professor at what is now Lexington Theological Seminary and at the University of Chicago Divinity School, Professor Bower came back to Lexington during his retirement. He called his retirement "retreading" because he got involved in so many new ventures. He wrote several books and he learned to paint. He sketched all of the scenes which were made into stained-glass windows of the Cane Ridge Shrine which covers the old Cane Ridge Meeting House where one important phase of the Christian Church (Disciples of Christ) was born. I did not know Professor Bower until he moved back to Lexington, but I cherished every minute I had a chance to be with him. It was often a delight for my wife and me to take him home from church on Sunday. He was always telling us of some new project he had just started or relating one of his anecdotes. He was past eighty then.

Until now I have not used the word "leisure." It has been deliberate. If I had not read Stephen C. Rose's chapter on "Saying Yes to Leisure" I probably would have used the word a number of times by now. Rose broadens and deepens the concept of leisure in the following:

Leisure is *not* the opposite of work. In many ways, the leisure revolution is as relevant to the world of the job, the occupation, as it is to the world of free time. For, in the deepest sense, leisure is whatever involves us, excites us, and brings out our interests and abilities; leisure

---

44. Trueblood, *The Common Ventures of Life,* p. 93f

exists only to the extent that we are *freely engaged* in what we are doing. . . .

What then is leisure? It is the free engagement of the individual with whatever moves him toward self-realization . . .

. . . Yes, leisure is a matter of inner attitude.[45]

If I understand his thesis, it is akin to the uses of time which Rollo May has described and which we quoted earlier in this chapter and in chapter four. It seems to me to mean that with all of the free time coming to us—free from work and in retirement—*time will take on new dimensions of trusteeship.* We will be blessed or cursed by what we do with it. We will be blessed if we see time as an opportunity for developing our abilities, our total gifts of life from God for growing in mind, body, and spirit into whole persons—persons who work, learn, play, share life with others for the joy and fulfillment of all. Then Stephen Rose adds:

The alternative . . . might well be the mass distribution of tranquilizers to dull the nation's fear of the awesome weight of unfilled hours. Along with this, there would have to be a refinement and expansion of radio and television so that scarcely a moment would pass without some diversion to remove from man's mind the suspicion that he is a man rather than a piano key. Some totalitarian government, a George Orwell, *1984,* incarnation of Big Brother, might succeed in producing a new slavery. Instead of real work, there could be make-believe work. We would become like the captured squirrels in their circular mesh cages, who run constantly, and yet remain stationary. In short, we would find a way to fill our time and, simultaneously, to avoid leisure.[46]

Not a pretty picture, is it? But surely a possible one. The only reason it does not frighten me is that I affirm my trusteeship of life which includes my trusteeship of time, and I vow that I will accept my part of the responsibility for it.

I once visited an elderly lady to talk with her about making a substantial gift to the seminary of which I was vice-president. I had visited her often, but on that day I learned that she had had cancer surgery and was not recovering very rapidly. I decided, because of her condition, not to mention the main purpose of my visit.

---

45. Rose, *Who's Killing the Church?* pp. 96-97.
46. *Ibid.,* p. 99.

She told me she was angry with her attorney because he advised her not to put in her will a number of specific bequests of pieces of furniture which had been in her family for a long time. He said that she should simply make a list of these bequests and file them along with her will, and that way her will would not be "cluttered" with such minute details. She said she was going to retain another attorney who would do what she wanted to do.

Then she said: "I've also decided to leave a substantial portion of my estate to my church and to our seminary."

"You know," she added, "that way, after I'm gone, I'll still be a part of the Lord's work here at home and in all the places where the seminary graduates are at work."

Writing a will took on new meaning for me that day. It is a way of adding a further dimension to the trusteeship of time and the trusteeship of our whole life.

A will is more than a mere legal instrument by which we dispose of property. It can be a "testament" through which we commit ourselves, in perpetuity, to that which we value most.

twelve

A Parable About Opportunity

"It's like a businessman who was leaving town for a long time and called in his assistants and turned over his investments to them. He made one responsible for about five hundred thousand dollars, another two hundred thousand, and another a hundred thousand—*according to each one's ability*—and then he left town. Right away the man with the five hundred grand got to work and made five hundred more. The man with the two hundred grand did the same and made another two hundred. But the guy with the hundred G's went and rented a safe-deposit box and put his boss' money in it. After a long time the boss returned and called his assistants together for an accounting. The one with the five hundred thousand brought his other five hundred thousand and said, 'Sir, you let me have five hundred grand; look, I've made another five hundred.' The boss said, 'Splendid, you good and responsible worker! You were diligent with the smaller sum; I'll entrust you with a larger one. You'll be a partner in my business.' Then the one with the two hundred G's came and said, 'Sir, you let me have two hundred thousand; look, I've made another two hundred.' The boss said, 'Splendid, you good and responsible worker! You were diligent with the smaller sum; I'll entrust you with a larger one. You'll be a partner in my business.' Well, the hundred-grand man came up and said, 'Sir, I know you are a hard-nosed man, squeezing pennies you haven't yet made and expecting a profit before the ink has dried. I was plain scared to take any chances, so I rented a safe-deposit box and put your money in it. Look, you've got every cent.' But his boss replied, 'You sorry, ornery bum! You knew that I squeeze pennies I haven't yet made, and expect profits before the ink dries. Then you should have turned my money over to the bank so that upon my return I would get back at least my principal with interest. So then, y'all take the money away from him and give it to the one with the million. For it will be given to everyone who has the stuff, and he'll have plenty, but the man who doesn't have the stuff will have even what he has taken away from him. Now as for this useless critter, throw him in the back alley. That'll give him something to moan and groan about.' "[47]

This parable of Jesus, found in Matthew 25:14-30, says more about *trusteeship* than any other recorded statement that he made. It has traditionally been called the "parable of the talents," since the traditional translations use the word "talents" as the designation of the sums which were given to the trustees. A talent was a measure of weight in its original usage but later came to mean a more specific amount of silver or gold. Goodspeed's translation suggests a value of about $1,000.00. At some time it may have been used as the name of a specific coin of about that value.

Luke records the same parable in a slightly different form in chapter 19:12-27, but instead of "talents" he speaks of *pounds,* and ten servants are entrusted with the sums. The word used in Luke, translated pounds, was *mina* which was worth about twenty dollars.

The English essayist, Thomas B. Macaulay, is said to be the first person to call attention to the fact that it is this parable which brought the word "talent" into the English language as a synonym for "ability" as in a "talent" for writing, singing, or so forth.

New Testament scholars have had difficulty in handling the verse which says, "For to every one who has will more be given,

---

47. Clarence Jordan, *The Cotton Patch Version of Matthew and John* (New York: Association Press, 1960), pp. 83-84. Used by permission.

and he will have abundance; but from him who has not, even what he has will be taken away," in Matthew 25:29. Some think that it was added to the original statement of Jesus, but Luke includes it in Luke 19:26 and in another setting in Luke 12:48b: ". . . Every one to whom much is given, of him will much be required; and of him to whom men commit much they will demand the more."

In Mark 4:25 we find: "For to him who has will more be given; and from him who has not, even what he has will be taken away." Again, in Luke 8:18 we read: "Take heed then how you hear; for to him who has will more be given, and from him who has not, even what he thinks he has will be taken away."

As a proverb of Jesus in some form the statement seems to be authentic; whether or not it belongs in Matthew 25:29 is at least to a degree, irrelevant. The fact that it is a kind of proverb from the lips of Jesus gives it credibility.

The key verse in the parable, it seems to me, is Matthew 25:15b: " . . . *to each according to his ability . . .* " This phrase indicates that this is *not* a parable about *talents as abilities* but about the trusteeship or the *use of abilities;* it is a *parable about opportunities to use abilities.* It doesn't make sense to me for Jesus to have said something about giving abilities to use abilities. But it does make sense to hear him saying something about opportunities to use abilities. One person had five opportunities, another had two opportunities, and another had one opportunity to use whatever abilities with which he was endowed. *Opportunities are a trusteeship.* Whether in this context or not, it makes sense to hear Jesus saying: "For to every one who has (opportunity) will more (opportunity) be given, and he will have (opportunity in) abundance; but from him that has not (opportunity), even what he has will be taken away."

This interpretation of the parable helps us to understand why the master (in the parable) treats his servants (trustees) as he does. In fact, it is the master's manner of dealing with the servants at the end of the parable, along with the key phrase noted above, that leads us to conclude that this is a parable about opportunity. It takes away from the master the role of an unusually hard taskmaster. He becomes one who only reminds the "wicked and slothful servant" that he has brought judgment upon himself; he simply suffers the consequences of his burying his one oppor-

tunity—throwing away his one chance—and his punishment is
due to his lack of responsibility.

Norman Cousins says in his "Author's Note" at the beginning
of his book, *The Celebration of Life,* that "A more precise title
for this book might be "Consequentialism.""[48] Toward the end of
the book he says:

Consequences give reality to man's capacity to struggle between good
and evil, nobility and venality, altruism and selfishness. A human being
fashions his consequences as surely as he fashions his goods or his
dwellings. Nothing that he says, thinks, or does is without its consequences. Just as there is no loss of basic energy in the universe, so no
thought or action is without its effects, present or ultimate, seen or un-
seen, felt or unfelt. Reality *is* consequences. . . . In short, life is of con-
sequence—literally so.[49]

That is not putting it too strongly for me, for I have found
consequences to be equally real.

Consequences come as the result of both our use of or failure to
use opportunities. Each generation and each person have unique
opportunities which come to them. At the close of World War I
we had such an opportunity in the League of Nations. Woodrow
Wilson saw its possibilities for peace and dedicated himself to its
establishment. Most of his American contemporaries, however,
thought him a foolish dreamer, not a realist. In due time came
World War II. Afterward history gave us a second chance. We
now have the United Nations and although it had warded off
World War III many times there are some skeptics who still do
not believe that it is better to battle with words than with bombs.
A few more have become a little more convinced after seeing the
results of Hiroshima and Nagasaki thirty years later. They are
learning for real that there is no place to hide.

In the church today we have another unique opportunity. It is
the Consultation on Church Union, an opportunity to create a
church that brings together the best of the traditions and energies
of a number of Protestant denominations into a church that
recognizes its trusteeship and servanthood instead of dissipating
its energies on the minutiae of organization and the trivia of
hierarchies. Who knows, with the present cooperation of
Protestants and Roman Catholics, we might even span that

---

48. Cousins, *The Celebration of Life,* p. vii
49. *Ibid.,* p. 77.

barrier of nearly half a millennium. Even if we fail to achieve all we hope for, we will have become better trustees of the faith for having tried. We will at least know why we are divided and will have found some better means of sharing the faith.

At this moment we are feeling the consequences of our poor trusteeship of the earth's resources in our present energy crisis. We have known it was coming for decades, but we did not listen to the true prophets of conservation. They warned us of the consequences of our wastefulness. But we still drive gas hogs on land, sea, and in the air and waste energy lighting up billboards telling us how much better one deodorant is than another. "Planned obsolescence" continues and we take pride in being "wastemakers," because we live in the "land of plenty" where wastemaking is a status symbol.

We hear the music, but do we ever listen, *really* listen and *really* hear the words of our contemporary rock prophets like Bob Dylan?

How many roads must a man walk down
Before you call him a man?
Yes, 'n' how many seas must a white dove sail
Before she sleeps in the sand?
Yes, 'n' how many times must the cannon balls fly
Before they're forever banned?
The answer, my friend, is blowin' in the wind,
The answer is blowin' in the wind.

How many times must a man look up
Before he can see the sky?
Yes, 'n' how many ears must one man have
Before he can hear people cry?
Yes, 'n' how many deaths will it take till he knows
That too many people have died?
The answer, my friend, is blowin' in the wind,
The answer is blowin' in the wind.
How many years can a mountain exist
Before it's washed to the sea?
Yes, 'n' how many years can some people exist
Before they're allowed to be free?
Yes, 'n' how many times can a man turn his head
Pretending he just doesn't see?

The answer, my friend, is blowin' in the wind,
The answer is blowin' in the wind.[50]

Karl Menninger, in his *Whatever Became of Sin?* has made a significant contribution to our understanding most of the ills that beset our culture and makes some concrete suggestions about what we can do about them. He writes from his point of view as a psychiatrist and as a churchman. If I understand what he is saying, after cataloguing the sins that are tearing asunder the fabric of our society and destroying us as persons, he makes a plea for all of us to be *concerned* about what besets us; to *care* more than we do about each other and to seek to overcome our *indifference*. He makes a special plea for clergymen, lawyers, judges, policemen, teachers, the media, statesmen, politicians, doctors, psychoanalysts—indeed *all of us*—to *be* the moral leaders that our times call for, in order to regain a moral stature and to be whole persons. I agree wholeheartedly with his thesis and I am grateful to him for his incisive analysis of our problems and his passion for seeking solutions. My only question after reading his book is not a question directed to him, but to myself and to all of us. *Will* we do it? *Can* we do it?

I can answer only for myself . . . We can and we will *IF* WE AFFIRM OUR TRUSTEESHIP AND ACCEPT OUR PERSONAL RESPONSIBILITIES AS TRUSTEES.

In the parable what was the major difference between the trustworthy trustees and the "wicked and slothful" trustee? Was it not that the former were *willing to risk?*

Human beings are strange creatures. We are willing to risk day after day for *things,* for material values, but most of us are loathe to risk for moral and spiritual values. We think nothing of obligating ourselves almost to the point of stupidity to buy houses, automobiles, washing machines, television sets, clothes, vacations, and even church buildings, but we are willing to invest very little of our time, our talents, our energies, our lives for the well-being of persons, for conserving and expanding rather than wasting all of the gifts of God.

To make possible wholeness for all persons means that we must be willing to take the risk of sharing with others who we

---

really are, not just who we appear to be. I have seen that kind of
risk take place in small groups and the results have been
miraculous. I was once a part of a small group where for days a
young woman struggled to share with the group a burden of guilt
which had been eating away at her life for nearly eight years.
Finally one day she shared her guilt with the group because she
had discovered that we love her and care for her; she had learned
that our love and care were far stronger and deeper than her feeling of guilt. So she "let it all hang out," and she found release.
She was willing to risk because we love her. But her willingness
to risk was helpful not only to her: we all grew ten feet tall
because she did.

That is the kind of risking that it takes to help us all put it all
together and to become the kinds of persons God wants us to be.

We aren't the only ones who take risks. God takes a risk with
every one of us. He has put the whole world in our hands as his
trustees. He trusts us to be trustworthy trustees, to accept the
gifts of life with gratitude and with responsibility.

Out of the hell of Auschwitz and Dachau and by using the gifts
of reason and will which God gave him, Viktor Frankl says:

What was really needed was a fundamental change in our attitude
toward life. We had to learn ourselves and, furthermore, we had to
teach the despairing men, that *it did not really matter what we expected
from life, but rather what life expected from us.* We needed to stop asking about the meaning of life, and instead to think of ourselves as those
who were being questioned by life—daily and hourly. Our answer must
consist, not in talk and meditation, but in right action and in right con-
duct. Life ultimately means taking the responsibility to find the right
answer to its problems and to fulfill the tasks which it constantly sets
for each individual.[51]

I pray that the rest of us will not be forced to endure other experiences of Auschwitz and Dachau to learn what life expects
from us, but that we will accept life for what it is, a gift from God
and that through our trusteeship we show him that we are
worthy of it.

---

51. Frankl, *Man's Search for Meaning,* ©1959, 1962 by Viktor Frankl. p. 77.

epilogue

God Could Have Made a Lot of Things

God could have made a lot of things instead of man;
He could have made a thousand things to fit his plan—
He could have made a robot out of flesh and blood,
Just wound him up, so that he'd unwind good.
He could have given a horse a mind to think and plan,
And made him keeper of the earth instead of man.

In the beginning God created the heavens and the earth. . . .
And God said, "Let there be light," and there was light.
And God saw that the light was good. . . .
God called the dry land Earth; and the waters that were gathered
  together he called Seas.
And God saw that it was good.
And God said, "Let the earth put forth vegetation, plants yielding seed,

and fruit trees bearing fruit in which is their seed, each according to
its kind, upon the earth."
And it was so. . . .
And God saw that it was good .
And God said, "Let there be lights in the firmament of the heavens to
separate the day from the night;
And let them be for signs and for seasons and for days and years, and let
them be lights in the firmament of the heavens to give light upon the
earth."
And it was so. . . .
And God said, "Let the waters bring forth swarms of living creatures,
and let birds fly above the earth across the firmament of the
heavens."
Then God said, "Let us make man in our image, after our likeness; and
let them have dominion over the fish of the sea, and over the birds of
the air, and over cattle, and over all the earth, and over every creep-
ing thing that creeps upon the earth."
So God created man in his own image, in the image of God he created
him; male and female he created them.
And God blessed them. . . .
And God saw everything that he had made, and behold, it was very
good. . . .[52]

The earth God made to be a storehouse full
Of things that could be used by everyone
To make the world a little bit of heaven.
When God looked 'round and saw what he had done
He gloried in the wisdom of his choice.
No robot could have satisfied his wish
To make a creature worthy of a voice
In ruling earth and her vast store of wealth.

For in his wisdom God worked hard and long
To make a creature that would be
His helper in the trusteeship of earth . . .
So one was born at the dawn of eternity.

And God was glad. He had a trustee now
To help him in his universal task.

---

52. Genesis 1.

He called him "man," and though man didn't ask
That it be so, God called him "son."

Thus at the very start of things, you see,
Were God and man and earth and everything
To make his plan what God would have it be.
But then—

A brother slays a brother in his greed—
The earth is blotted first with stain of blood

A thousand armies march across the plains—
A million people die from lack of food.

A thousand years of slavery and strife—
The earth is desecrated once again.

The earth that once was God's, so clean and neat,
Becomes a heap of rubbish at his feet.

The righteous sole for silver on the block
The needy auctioned for a pair of shoes.

The temple used for bartering and trade—
"And God saw everything that he had made."

Did God think then that all he made was good?
He could have made a robot out of flesh and blood;
He could have made a lot of things instead of man;
He could have made a thousand things to fit his plan . . .
But he didn't, see—
He made you and he made me.

We're all he has to make his plan complete—
To take his earth, to make it clean and neat
To change it from a place of blood and tears
To one devoid of pain and death and fears.

It's trusteeship, this life of ours he's given
To make the earth a little nearer heaven . . .

It's Time, this trusteeship
   Time in which to do his will;
   Time to make the most of while we're here;
   Time to teach a child to grow like him;
   Time for families where God is near.

It's Talent, too, this trusteeship—
   Talent used, not merely buried;
   Talent to conserve and build up earth;
   Talent to sing and teach and share;
   To thank God for and prove one's worth.

It's work, this trusteeship—
   Honest business, truly spent;
   Serving others, not oneself alone—
   Working with a joyous zest,
   Not as an automated drone.

It's Possessions, this trusteeship—
   Gifts to persons, truly shared,
   With those who cry alone in need;
   Not hoarded as a miser hoards,
   Fondling his treasure in his greed.

It's Money, this trusteeship—
   Money as the symbol of life;
   Money that we cannot borrow—
   But life that's spent; invested in
   What life can bring to all tomorrow.

We're all he has to make his plan complete—
To take his earth and make it clean and neat;
To change it from a place of blood and tears
To one of his design throughout the years . . .

God could have made a lot of things instead of man;
He could have made a thousand things to fit his plan.
But he didn't, see—
He made you and he made me!

90

Addendum

It has been suggested that I write this addendum to suggest various ways in which this book might be used. I am happy to do so, although my purpose in writing it has not been to produce a "study guide," but a book to be *experienced* by the reader. Its style is not that of providing content although it obviously contains some information. Rather, I hope that the individual reader and groups using it will view it as a dialogue between the author and the persons who read it. It was not written as an "I-you" (author and reader) book, but a "we" book, with the author and reader sharing the experience of searching for life meaning.

As you read *God's Trustees,* I hope you will literally "talk back" to me out loud, reacting to what I am sharing, recalling similar or different ideas and experiences which you have had. By doing so you will be able to identify with what I am sharing with you and thereby grow in your own life experiences.

You may want to use *God's Trustees* as a resource in small groups—growth groups, peer-colleague clusters of ministers, church school classes, church committees on membership development, evangelism, stewardship, youth or adult fellowship groups, prayer groups, church boards, etc. It would be fun to use it as a resource for persons who bring their lunches to work, eat together, and have "bull sessions" over coffee. It might be grist for college or seminary klatches. As you read it, decide for yourself how it might be utilized to stimulate sharing experiences with other persons. I firmly believe that the *process* of sharing in a group is often more helpful than *what* is shared.

If you and others with whom you associate decide to use it as a resource, *God's Trustees* lends itself to an experiment in shared leadership. Rather than having one person serve as a discussion leader, agree to have someone serve as convenor of the group and allow various persons in the group who identify with an idea, an illustration or maybe with an entire chapter, to share their identification or reaction with the other persons present. What the group experiences and shares will probably be even more meaningful than the book itself.

Your group might want to try role-playing some of the material presented, especially that in the chapters on communities of trustees, or to practice various communication models such as "active listening" or sending "I messages" mentioned in the chapter on words.

It has been my experience that in any group of people, each has much to learn from others in the group. Read *God's Trustees,* share it with others, and *do your own thing*. It will be fun and each of you will learn something—maybe from the book—but surely from each other.